Unapologetically Woman

A Woman without Regrets or Excuses

EJF Publishing & Printing
Hillside, IL 60162

Copyright© 2009 by Unapologetically Woman

All rights reserved. No part of this book may ever be used or reproduced in any manner whatsoever without written permission except in the case of brief quotations embodied in critical articles and reviews. Although the authors and publishers have made every effort to ensure the accuracy and completeness of the information contained in this book, we assume no responsibility for errors, inaccuracies, omissions, or any inconsistency therein.

Any slights of people, places, belief systems or organizations are unintentional. Any resemblance to anyone living deceased or somewhere in between is truly coincidental.

**For more information and additional copies, contact:
EJF Publishing & Printing
contact@ejfpublish.com**

Printed in the United States of America by:
EJF Publishing and Printing
2205 S Wolf Rd. Suite 151
Hillside, Illinois 60162
http://www.ejfpublish.com/

ISBN-13 978-0-9841797-1-8

Cover Design Concept EJF Publishing & Printing
Cover Designed by Designs by Christina
Interior Layout by EJF Publishing & Printing and
Shadrina F. Fleming - Fleming Admin Works

Unless otherwise indicated, all scriptural quotations are taken from the King James Version of the Bible or the New International King James Version.

This Project is Dedicated

To My Sister,
Fertamia (Tammy) Smith

Dear Unapologetically Woman Tammy,

Watching you journey into womanhood, I never could have imagined the tower of strength your presence would yield. Your tenacity to live outside of the walls of abuse, ridicule, shame, and manipulation is worthy to be noted…

I miss you more than you know.

The love and strength you poured into your children as a single mother will never be forgotten!

In one of our last conversations, you told me that I am "Unapologetically Woman too."

Thank you for causing me to remember!

Love, Desi

Foreword

I am pleased to recommend this treasury of goodness and blessing which applauds the strength, tenacity, and the unquenchable spirit of women. The truth is that women have always persevered to sustain their families and communities. With grace, they have nurtured children, loved husbands, cared for the elderly, and worked long hours (whether at home or on a job). They have met with difficulties and managed serious problems. They have battled for what they believe in and have denied themselves for the sake of others. At the same time, women have suffered their share of heartaches and pain. Sometimes they have gone unrecognized, unappreciated, and unloved. Unfortunately, some have been victimized by violence and even lost their lives. In this book, **Unapologetically Woman,** you will find the stories of women which reflect this diversity of the human experience.

Women of different ages, ethnicities, and backgrounds have collaborated to tell their powerful, true stories in this book. You will see how they have grappled with issues of identity, self-esteem, healthy friendships, violence, sexual abuse, grief, faith, forgiveness, disappointments, and hope. Woven throughout the tapestry of their experiences are threads of faith which hold together, strengthen, and reinforce the fiber of their lives. What is most exciting is that these women have triumphed over difficult circumstances to arrive at where they are today.

We have long needed a book like this and I am so glad to witness the labor of love that has produced this compelling volume. Truly, these authors have given the reader a priceless treasure. I invite you to peruse its contents and absorb its insights…imbibe its sensibilities. Read it thoroughly and enjoy its miraculous wonders and testimonies. Be encouraged, be inspired, and open your heart to the wonder of God's power to transform lives and bring us back from setbacks. These women will inspire you to stand up for what you believe and to believe in what you stand for *unapologetically*. More importantly, they will remind you that in spite of life's challenging and painful experiences, you can always find the strength to rise up and stand tall. In the end, worship the Lord in the beauty of His holiness for bringing this ensemble of godly women authors together for such a time as this.

Juliet Allen
Contributing Author

Table of Contents

Foreword..v

Introduction to Unapologetically Woman........................9

Section One..15

    You Can Make It Happen....................................15

        HELLO—Life is Calling!...............................21

        In Realizing Me..34

Section Two..36

    Friends and Relationships..................................36

        Uh, Uh, Not This Time!...............................39

        Friendship at its Purest................................59

Section Three..71

    Who's That Woman in the Mirror?.......................71

        Who Am I?..75

        THE QUEEN OF COMEBACK....................85

    Reflections by Fertamia (Tammy) Smith................99

Section Four 102

The Power of Life in Spite of My Right Now! 102

- I Can Breathe Again 105
- Trial by Fire 121
- Against All Odds 133
- *No More Regrets* 142
- Collaboration Package 147

Introduction to Unapologetically Woman
A Woman without Regrets or Excuses!

Ladies, life always moves on and every girl child eventually grows into a woman. While a girl does not choose whether she wants to become a woman, she does have a say about the kind of woman she chooses to become. The reality is choices come a dime a dozen and many women struggle with making healthy choices that complement, enhance, or empower their lives. You name it, you know it, women have had to deal with it—stress, demands, disappointments, frustrations, betrayals, regrets, and even violence. This book features the personal stories of eight women who have gained wisdom through struggles, heartbreak, pain, and setbacks. Each story is one of triumph because all these women have learned the secret of being themselves, unapologetically.

Today, you too can choose to become an unapologetic woman. There is no more time for making excuses about what parents, spouses, teachers, siblings, did or did not do. You must take responsibility and live life forward with courage and determination. The intention of this book is not to minimize your problems and struggles but to help shift your focus to see yourself moving beyond where you are so you can get to the next level. Constantly reliving the pain and hurts of yesterday is unfruitful and hinders progress today and tomorrow. Be encouraged to love yourself enough to forgive and move on with your life. Are you ready to move forward?

To begin, I invite you to read the fascinating collection of stories by everyday women in this book; filled with inspiration and guidance, these women unveil their personal limitations, struggles, relationship failures, and comebacks. Their stories will empower you if you are one of those women who may be tired of being the odd woman out. These women want you to know that it is time to give up the regrets and excuses because self-sabotage is no longer an option. If you have ever felt different, or wished you had made better decisions, then this is the book for you. Learn how real women have dealt with a wide range of issues and gain insight for your life through reading this collection.

The good news is that being "unapologetically woman" is not a club you join but a lifestyle you embrace. It is not about being loud, obnoxious, ignorant, flamboyant, snappy, rude, or unable to apologize for wrongdoings. It is finding strength from within, without regrets. When obstacles appear, it is having courage to move beyond them. It is bouncing back after hitting rock bottom. It is being resilient and confident in one's own accomplishments. It is refusing to let poverty and circumstances hold you back from what you are capable of accomplishing. It is having the beauty, which comes from the inside out and exuding that beautiful, strength and courage in your daily life.

Being an unapologetic woman has its costs. It may cost you some friendships and it may also cost giving up the false image you project to the world. It does require that you be authentic and not allow others to define you. You do not need to become a "clone" of someone you respect or look up to, just because you admire them. Never allow yourself to become frustrated trying to conform to the expectations of other women or men. Be true to yourself and showcase the uniqueness and beauty of your own design. Open your eyes and see who God truly created you to be and imagine the impact of being your authentic self will have on others! You have the potential to make a real difference in this world. To tell you the truth, others are waiting on you to change, so they can change. You were created to help others move from sorrow to hope, but you can never accomplish this with an attitude of self-pity, a mindset of lack, or a spirit of frustration.

Be advised that having all the money and resources you want is not what qualifies you as an Unapologetic Woman. What qualifies you is your tenacity to persevere in life in spite of the scars, agony, sorrows of defeat, poverty, abandonment, lack, divorce, single parenting, rape, torment, and rejection. Your resilience, courage, and strength, will surely advance you to a place where your life story can positively influence others. I believe you are reading this book because you are predestined to be a woman of purpose who lives "without regrets or excuses". No matter what you are presently facing, nothing should stop you from being who God designed you to be.

In April of 2009, Tammy, one of my closest sisters was violently snatched from us. Her murder rocked me to the core. Losing her has been extremely difficult and painful and it has taken every ounce of strength to keep it together because I miss her so much. Sometimes when I think about her, the Lord reminds me of one of our last heart-to-heart conversations when Tammy challenged me to see myself not as a little girl victim but as a strong, unapologetic woman. She reminded me to live and not die and to always be intentional about pursuing destiny. What an encouragement it was to receive such a challenge from a strong young woman, who had her own share of pain in life. Surviving rape as a teenager and domestic violence as a single parent, Tammy was able to reach beyond the circumstances and speak life into me.

As time passes and her voice slowly fades, I appreciate her for pushing me to be me, with no apologies. Now, do not get me wrong, if I have wronged someone I know how to apologize. However, for me to make excuses for being a successful, creative, outspoken, and a beautiful African American woman of faith, I will not make any apologies! My scars have qualified me to walk unapologetically as a strong woman; I do not just say it I now live it! I do so with the urgency of a person emerging from a coma after five or ten years. It would be unimaginable not to celebrate life after enduring such a loss of time. Just as that person certainly needs to move beyond what they went through, I believe we all need to leave our past behind and reach towards our futures with unyielding passion. We may not be able change what happened to us five or ten years ago or even yesterday, but we all have the right and power to change what happens today and beyond.

Every woman's journey is different but every woman has the opportunity to choose the path her life will take. For example, say you decide that today I am going to get up early enough to spend time in mediation with the Lord, exercise, get dressed, eat breakfast with a loved one, and so forth. There is a good chance it will happen because "YOU" put it into place. First, you speak it and then you act. Proverbs 18:21 confirms, "The tongue has the power of life and death." It begins with the words of your mouth, followed by your actions that your plans are put into motion.

You see, being unapologetically woman, is not whether you are a particular race, age, or from a certain background. It is the essence of who you are. From your core flows charisma, excellence, intelligence, courage, faith, hope, healing, and strength. You have to tap into who you are, in order for you to be embrace WHOSE you are. We belong to someone greater than ourselves. We did not make ourselves so even when our best feelings are not good enough, we can relinquish it to God. We may not look like a polished diamond or gold rings and we might have several flaws, but when we turn our lives over to Him, He can work miracles. He is a master at taking our weaknesses, scars, pains, sadness, and junk, and transforming our situation for the better. He promises that He can make everything work together for our good if we only trust in Him.

He can even turn our mourning into dancing and our sorrow into laughter according to Psalms 30:11. In my own life, I am learning to smile again after the death of my sister. The pain was so great when Tammy passed that I thought I would never smile again, let alone live. I felt it would not be fair to smile and enjoy my life because she was no longer here for us to enjoy her beautiful smile and life. However, God is comforting me and giving me strength even in this great sorrow. He has given me this opportunity to tell you that there is nothing you have been through so tragic that He cannot heal. You can be free to live again.

In closing, I dare you to embrace the essence of who you are. Begin canceling the words that others have spoken over you and begin to take back your life. Be the woman that you know you are. No matter what time in your life you are reading this book, change can happen today. Now is your time, you can decide to become a strong, empowering and wonderful unapologetic woman today!

Sincerely,

Desiree Fleming (Lady Des)
Editor in Chief
EJF Publishing & Printing

> *"The words pinned by Desiree Fleming, as well as the other talented writers, in "Unapologetically Woman" are compelling and most certainly thought-provoking. I am challenged to continue to be creative, charismatic, and so much more! You will be enlightened and challenged as well. What an honor given to the memory Desiree's precious sister, Tammy. Her legacy will live on through this piece of work."*
>
> *Pastor Gloria Alford*
> *Progressive Life Cathedral Word Cathedral*

Section One
You Can Make It Happen

I am "Unapologetically Woman"

A Woman without Regrets or Excuses!
An Affirmation Stance

By Desiree Fleming

I make no apologies for being me, because I was created for this very purpose!

For one to say I was a "Mistake" is a "Mistake!" Being me is being free to Love, Share, Embrace, and Celebrate Life!

Being anything else but me, Is Apologetic!

I am "Unapologetically Woman"

Learning to accept me in the beginning was difficult!

But, once I got to know and love me, I had No Regrets!

Oh yeah, the rumor was I wouldn't "Survive"

Un-employed! Divorced! Widowed! Single Mom!

Too much success! Not enough!

But, did you forget…

You cannot stop what I was Destined to be!

I am UN-Stoppable! I am UN-Quenchable! I am UN-Movable!

I am "Unapologetically Woman"

Yes, you're right, I'm overweight, but Beautiful! Thin, but Intelligent! Weak, but Strong! Gentle but Fierce!

And yes, fear grips me from time to time because of the unknown, But, I know for certain, it won't last too long!

To be me is unusual! You ask me why…I'll tell you why…

NO one can Walk like me! NO one can Talk like me! NO one can Love like me! NO one can Pray like me!

NO one can Give like me! Absolutely, NO one can Be me!

WHY? Because,

"I am Unapologetically Woman"

Foreword for Juliet Allen

Ours is a very challenging era for women. Faced with changing definitions or expressions of femininity, the perils and possibilities of womanhood, plus all the demands of marriage, family and career, life has always been tricky for astute godly women. It is a wonder they contribute so much to church and society. Truly, their sacrificial love to family and faith community is commendable [Psalms 126:5]. I have seen the qualities of a virtuous woman up close and personal in the love of my wife and it is my joy to write this foreword for her chapter.

Juliet reminds us all that life is an adventure made more meaningful with a personal faith in Jesus Christ. I can attest that her stories bear testimony to the power of God to sustain our lives in good times and bad. After more than thirty years of marriage, I am very proud that she is writing out of the overflow of her life experience. Her characteristic energy, enthusiasm, and optimism consistently add zest and joy to our home. I am blessed by her thoughtfulness and nurtured by her care. She is truly a treasure.

I hope that her chapter inspires generations of women and men alike to embrace life with faith, hope, and love. Indeed, life is calling and every day is another step along the journey. May we rise to the challenge to live purposefully and renew our commitment to repair the breaches in our lives, families, and communities [Isaiah 58].

Dr. Henry L Allen
Wheaton College
Wheaton, IL

Juliet Allen

Juliet is a passionate believer that every life has a purpose and a story. The Founder of Keepsake Creations, Juliet enjoys using her creativity to design and create memory books, which chronicle and celebrate life stories.

A gifted writer and editor, Juliet has been published in several venues including ministry publications of Mainstay Church Resources and a national book of poetry. Currently, she is a regular contributor to her church's newsletter, Joyful Noise. Articulate and inspirational, Juliet speaks at churches, women events, and regularly teaches at a weekly women's Bible study. She is a dedicated Christian Education team leader, teacher, and the Director of Easter programming at her home church, Jubilee Baptist in Bolingbrook, IL. Juliet serves on the Executive Board of the African American Leadership Roundtable, Inc. in the western suburbs of Chicago where she is an active community leader. Currently, she works for Integrated Technology and Business Services in Naperville, Illinois.

Originally from Liberia, West Africa, Juliet has lived in the United States for the last thirty-two years. She attended

Wheaton College and graduated summa cum laude from Bethel University, St Paul, Minnesota with her Bachelor of Arts degree in Sociology. She is married to Dr. Henry L. Allen, Chair of the Sociology and Anthropology Department at Wheaton College and lives in Wheaton, Illinois. Together they have eight children: Jonathan, Jessica, Janice, Justin, Julia, Janel, Joseph, Judith and one granddaughter, Ava Jordyn Isabel.

HELLO—Life is Calling!
By Juliet Allen

Every morning I wake up and I say to myself: "Listen up—Life is calling! You have the gift of another day, what will you do with it? Are you ready to grow, change, and become all that God had in mind when He created you?" Immediately, I want my response to be "Yes! Yes! Yes!" My heart's desire is to have a positive attitude and to make my daily journey a faith-filled adventure. I want to keep going and growing because I know God has so much more in store for me. Yet sometimes, I get frustrated when the going gets tough—problems overwhelm, money gets tight, and tensions erupt in my marriage. In those moments when disappointments and setbacks come uninvited, facing life with a positive attitude can be challenging. I always have to go back to the verse in Jeremiah 29: 11 to remember that no matter what I am facing, God's plans for me are good, He wants to give me a future and a hope.

Along the way, I have to keep reminding myself of the greatness of God. Things may look bleak now but He is going to work it out for my good. I may be sowing in tears but He will cause me to reap with joy! No mountain of difficulty I face is greater than my God who can move any mountains. By shifting my focus from how big my problems are to God who is far bigger, I can have the confidence that God will see me through. I have learned to say, "Alright God, I am going to put this item in your To Do box. I know I cannot handle it but you can! You can make a way when there seems to be no way."

Today, God has given me a determined mindset and courage to embrace life regardless. I believe that my best days are still ahead and that God has more good things in store for me (and you) than we can even imagine. When life calls, I remind myself of several important truths from scriptures and always challenge myself to take positive steps.

Life has purpose!

When I read Rick Warren's bestseller, *The Purpose Driven Life* (2002), a few years ago, I reflected on his provocative and inescapable question: "What on Earth Am I Here For?" He observed, "If you want to know why you are placed on this earth, you must begin with God. You were born by his purpose and for his purpose." I have discovered his conclusion to be true: "Without God, life has no purpose and without purpose, life has no meaning." Truly, my life has meaning and purpose because of my faith in God. I believe that God has made me with a unique personality and purpose...this is true for you too! We are all original creations from the mind of God; we are one-of-a-kind people. When God made you and me, He threw away the mold. It amazes me that even before I was born, God planted the seed of purpose in my life. No one has been exactly like me before nor will be like me in the future. My distinct talents, abilities, interests, and personality differentiate me from everyone else and equip me specifically for my life's purpose. God made me the way I am to achieve all He planned for me. As a result, I do not have to apologize to anyone for who I am. I am unapologetically woman because that is who God made me to be!

While reading Myles Munroe's book, *In Pursuit of Purpose* (1996), I was inspired by his argument that God has a special contribution for each of us here on this earth. How empowering to know that my very existence is proof that I have something unique to contribute. Having this perspective allows me to live intentionally. Knowing that God created and equipped me to do good works anchors my life like a strong foundation anchors a house—we dare not underestimate the value of a strong foundation! I am therefore reminded of the story Jesus told about two builders in the Gospel of Matthew. The foolish man built his house on the sand while the wise man built his house on the rock. When the storms raged, the foolish man's house collapsed but the wise man's house stood firm. Knowing that a weak foundation will always leave one vulnerable during the storms of life, I have chosen to build my life on the strong foundation of faith in Jesus Christ. This foundation has held me steady in the face of struggles that could have easily rocked my world and brought my house down. I know I am still standing today after the financial, marital, and parenting storms of my life because God brought me through it all. He has been there to sustain me when waves of adversity threatened to steal my joy. In the process, I have learned to stretch my faith.

Stretch my faith!

Once I came across this saying: "Faith can rewrite your future;" I know this to be true because it has happened to me. I once found myself in a situation where I was experiencing a total faith failure. My vision was limited to what I could see and I just did not know how our family was going to move forward in a particular circumstance. I had forgotten or, should I say, neglected to look to our mighty God who has the power to change any situation.

During the summer of 1986, I discovered I was expecting my fifth child; to be truthful I was not at all thrilled. My husband and I were living in Minnesota at the time and I was happy with our family size. In fact, I thought it was perfect—two boys and two girls—just what we hoped for when we got married. The unplanned pregnancy of a fifth child threw me for a loop because I had my own agenda in mind. I thought, "Not now!" Here I was on the threshold of completing my college degree in December and I was dreaming of the new changes ahead, not another child. At the time, my faith was not willing to accommodate the idea of another child in my "perfect life".

Throughout the pregnancy, God was working on my attitude, but I was a reluctant learner. One of my biggest concerns about having another child had to do with finances and I worried constantly about how we would survive. We needed extra income and I was not working, living on a single income was tough. In my mind's eye, all I could see were all the limitations, and I did not dwell on the ability of God to provide for our needs. Instead, I magnified my problems, completely forgetting that God is able to do exceedingly abundantly above all that I could ask for or think (Ephesians 3:20).

That year, God placed me in an "accelerated learning program" to enlarge my faith and expand my understanding of His purpose and power. Through a series of sermons, I got a new understanding of God's purpose and I learned that it is hidden in every child whether a pregnancy is planned or not. Sometimes, the unplanned and unexpected events of life lead to the greatest miracles and blessings. As for our family, I began to accept that God plans for me might be bigger than I had ever dreamed or imagined. I needed to trust that God was working things out even in this situation... what a thought! To my surprise, I discovered that God was well able to provide for our growing family. Through a series of ordained circumstances—I do not believe in coincidences—my husband connected with a high-ranking administrator from another college. A few conversations later, my husband was a candidate for a new and better paying job. By the time our daughter arrived in 1987, my husband was in the process of changing jobs—he had a job offer at a higher salary scale and academic rank in a totally different state. When fear and worries had overtaken me, God gave me a "faith lift". He showed me that He is able to do all things and bring about unanticipated endings. My future was being rewritten and my faith was growing. More than twenty years later, I now know that when I do not understand what is going on at the moment, I need to look at life beyond the moment. God is always at work and He is a master at turning what appears to be weakness into greatness and failure into victory. What a mighty God we serve!

Once I got out of a negative or fearful mindset, I was able to open my heart to God's bigger purposes for my life. With my faith stretched, I learned I could believe for more and reach for new heights. As it turns out, I had three more children after my crisis of faith over my fifth child. Years later, I would learn another lesson during a crisis.

Keep hope alive!

Have you noticed that as long as we are alive, we can never escape trouble? Trouble always seems to know how to find us. It does not matter how much money we have in our bank account, the kind of house we live in, our neighborhood, who our parents are, who we know, what kind of job you have, or anything else—trouble always comes knocking. If you do not believe it, pay attention to the news and watch people you know; eventually trouble arrives. It has found me on occasion and maybe it has found you too. Now when trouble surrounds me, I have learned to remind myself that it cannot defeat me because my hope is in God and hope makes a difference! In the darkest of times, hope keeps us going; without it, people die. Tom Rath and Donald Clifton described an interesting study by psychiatrist, Dr. William E. Mayer, in their book, *How Full is your Bucket?* (2004). Dr. Mayer, who later became the US Army's chief psychiatrist, noticed a disturbing pattern when a person loses hope. He studied American soldiers in the Korean POW Camp and discovered that although American soldiers were not subjected to routine physical torture in the camps, they were exposed to extreme mental torture at the hands of their captors. As a result of the mental torture tactics, soldiers were plagued by a disease of extreme hopelessness. The soldiers called it the "give up-itis" and surprisingly, they died from it as rapidly as if they had been exposed to a real physical ailment. Mayer observed that hopelessness—this ultimate weapon of war—caused the highest POW death rate in U.S. military history. If lacking hope is so disastrous, having hope must make a powerful difference because it allows us to see beyond our difficulties.

I cannot tell you how many crises, usually financial, that my husband and I have endured over the years; in every situation, we had to keep hope alive. When it seemed there was no way, God always made a way. Many times, it was not the time we expected or the way we imagined—in truth, it was always darkest before the dawn but we saw miracles come out of our difficulties.

I will always remember the time when we were literally between a rock and hard place. This time, it was 1997 and that April my husband received a new job offer. We were thrilled about this new opportunity. Since my husband is in academia, he specifically inquired as to when his contract would become effective because we needed income over the summer months. He was assured they would take care of it and there would be no lapse in his income. Well, two months later we found out otherwise, just what we feared indeed happened. His new contract would not be in force until September of that year, which meant that for the entire summer, we would have no money coming in...imagine that! Well, my husband and I were devastated. What would we do about our bills...how would we provide for our children? Could we survive with no regular income? We had no idea but we knew God had not brought us this far to abandon us, so we refused to lose hope.

We rejoiced that at least my husband had one source of income for that summer—a consulting contract to write an article. We knew however, that August was the earliest we could expect compensation since the article was not even written yet. All that summer, we watched our bank account hover on empty and our extremity became God's opportunity. Like Moses and the children of Israel facing the Red Sea, we were at the proverbial "wit's end." I heard someone say once, "When you are down to nothing, God is up to something." Every day I wondered… "What's up, God?" Yet, day by day He revealed that his mercy and faithfulness were new every morning. Creditors granted extensions on many of our bills, our Landlord deferred our rent payments and our two teenage children gave regularly and generously of their limited summer earnings to help see us through. Money was tight, but God was providing for us in daily increments.

When August arrived, we were still hanging in there. The title of a recent book by Cornel West accurately describes our situation at that time—*"Hope on a Tightrope!"* As a family, we prayed more than ever before. My husband had finally completed the article and we were eager for a quick turnaround on his consulting fees. We soon got word that his compensation had been approved and we were overjoyed. Buoyed by the good news, we could finally see light at the end of the tunnel! Then, for almost three weeks, there was no check in the mail. With September fast approaching and school right around the corner, I could not believe it took that long to mail a promised check. However, we were dealing with a bureaucracy and spiritual warfare. During the darkest hours, when my faith was at its lowest point, God sent us a miracle. I received a phone call from a wonderful old friend and at discovering our desperate plight, she quickly offered to loan us some money. In a matter of two days, we received a check via express mail for double the amount she had offered—what a blessing that was. The other check, my husband's fee, finally arrived several days later. This incidence of God's deliverance at the midnight hour has stayed with me all these years; it serves as a reminder that out of difficulties, miracles can and do happen.

It is good to know that trouble does not last always for if trouble does not break us, it makes us stronger. Troubles may come but God never intends for them to destroy us. Every athlete faces obstacles and challenges, but champions are those who overcome! God sees us as champions and He has made us to be victors not victims. He fashioned each one of us himself and deposits potential in us. According to Ephesians 2:8, I am God's masterpiece! A masterpiece is valuable and excellently crafted. It excites me to know that God made me and believes in me. Even when I have made a mess of things with poor choices, God is able and willing to refashion and repurpose me. I always have value to God, I am truly priceless for He has forgiven my past and created a new future for me. How encouraging to know that whenever we turn our lives over to God He is waiting to do something new in us. He is able to set us on a new path and unleash our hidden potential.

Unleash my Potential!

Years ago, I received a greeting card with the poem *Just Think*, by Roy Lessin the founder of Dayspring Cards. Some things will catch your eye in life, but his words caught my

Unapologetically Woman

heart: "Just think, you are not here by chance but by God's choosing, He has allowed you to be here at this time of history to fulfill His special purpose for this generation." I believe God has deposited potential in each of our lives, sometimes we use it, and sometimes we do not. Heaven forbid that we go to the grave without using all the potential stored in our lives! We need to seize opportunities to use our potential to touch the lives of others for the better. Just as a stone tossed into quiet lake creates a ripple, one life can make a huge difference. We will never know our impact until we unleash our potential and then the impact may be greater than we can ever imagine.

I discovered this firsthand in 2009 when I had a unique opportunity to coordinate my family reunion the affect I could have on others. For me, this was a chance to pursue a lifelong passion—explore my family's historical roots. In the end, it proved to be a divine assignment with historic significance for multiple generations of my extended family. Looking back, I marvel at how at the appointed time, I unleashed all my potential—my acquired skill sets and lifelong curiosities—to assume this leadership role. Only God knew that my interest in researching genealogy, reading biographies, studying African American history, documenting life stories, and a love of family would be just the components necessary to accomplish the task of reuniting family members to celebrate our family story. A story that dates back to 1829 when four Cooper brothers left Norfolk, Virginia on the ship *Harriet* en route to

You Can Make It Happen

Liberia, West Africa to escape slavery and build better lives for themselves. After 180 years, that reunion in Richmond, Virginia convened many of their descendants, several of whom were once again living in the United States, to celebrate heritage and God's faithfulness across the generations. What a joy it was for me to see an idea come to fruition. What's more, it confirmed the importance of how stepping up to utilize one's potential can make a huge difference. Moreover, just think, every day is another opportunity for us to do this.

Realize every day is a Gift

Each day I am alive, I know I have the gift of another twenty-four hours—what a gift filled with a world of opportunities! Just think—each day, I have the power and privilege to bless a child, a friend, a family member, and even my community. I have the chance to learn something new or embark on a new adventure. I can be an agent of change and the bearer of good news. I can make a real difference to somebody when life calls and you can too! Everyday counts and I am challenged to make each day good; to make every day good. Norman Vincent Peale once said, "We must think a good day, plan a good day, and pray a good day." I am so glad that I can make each day a new beginning no matter what happened the day before. I am grateful that God's faithfulness is new every morning and if I make a mistake, I can correct it. If I fall short of my goals, I can try again. If I am facing overwhelming odds, health challenges, financial setbacks, or relationship failures,

God is always there. He has the power to change my situation, but more importantly, He is able to transform the way I view my situation.

Life is calling every day, I encourage you to unwrap it as a gift! Today is the beginning of the rest of your life. Realize your purpose and stretch your faith because it is time to keep hope alive. Dare to dream and unleash your potential because I once heard "No one can predict to what heights you can soar until you spread your wings!" Life is shorter than we think but God has so much in store for us. Now is the time to make life count...are you ready? Life is calling you!

In Realizing Me
By Shadrina F. Fleming

So much of my identity is wrapped up in my success and failures to the extreme that one will invariably carry more weight

In turn, failures will consume my every emotions and waking thoughts and meager success will not prove desired relief

Brief spurts of presumed light will only serve to widen the void between despair and bliss and I will surely wonder… what's the point of all of this!

For hopelessness is at least a sign, that I am alive, breathing and feeling…right?

I am a woman in darkness, I suffer in silence. The transgressions against me have stolen my voice.

I try to bury these emotions that flood me, threatening to replace my fake smile for the outside world
With a deep wailing cry.

But there is an outpour of my spirit, a release…and I hear it!
It is Life Calling Me!

It is as if a soprano saxophone is playing the smooth rift to the music of my theme song.

Unapologetically Woman

I realize the possibilities, the realities of my strength
I recognize the darkness but it does not overcome me

My circumstances have no way to disenfranchise me, for I am diligent, a vigilante for my place and my rightful seat as an heir of royalty.

I grew up and played at the feet of mighty Queens, Warriors in the spiritual realm.

And they have prepared me, praying for me, they remind me

As I take back my voice, the darkness fades and the light of hope is blinding! I stand upright, whole-heartedly and strong

I accept my place as the next Queen to carry forth a generation, as my birthright explodes and spills across this page

I realize my destiny... I know that *I Can Make it Happen*!

Mother Maya says I am Phenomenal Woman but I am also

Unapologetic, Unapologetically,

Unapologetic Woman That's Me!

Section Two
Friends and Relationships

Foreword for Nicole Ross

Nicole Friday-Ross captures the transforming and oftentimes painful lessons that are associated with giving love without loving yourself in this captivating chapter. She shares her life-changing experience in an effort to enlighten women about the consequences of losing oneself in an unreciprocated love relationship. Nicole's detailed accounts of her past relationship is intended to encourage women to take a non-judgmental inventory of their own sense of self to determine how it is manifested in their intimate relationships. "Uh, Uh, Not This Time" is a story about love's challenges, hurts, and triumphs. But most of all, its message seeks to help women understand and embrace a kind of love that heals and never disappoints – the love of God…Agape love.

Gina Webster

Nicole Friday-Ross

Nicole is a resident of the far south suburbs of Chicago, where she was born and raised. A God fearing, virtuous woman, Nicole is married to an equally yoked husband, Ron, and they have a beautiful baby girl, Marsei´.

Nicole's first passion is music. With a highly attuned ear for harmony and a mega voice to-boot, Nicole and her husband were inspired to create God's Appointed Ministries in 2001. It has been said that they offer effortless vocal deliverance of praise and worship. These gifts have positioned them to hold significant roles with the Stellar Award-winning gospel group Shekinah Glory. Nicole and Ron contributed a powerful duet to their 2007 CD, simply titled "Lord You Are."

Nicole is also passionate about planning and she founded her own Event Planning business. An independent consultant, she has operated this successful business for over six years.

Uh, Uh, Not This Time!
By Nicole Friday-Ross

For many years, I was in an unhealthy relationship where I loved a man more than myself. I had been so fascinated and blinded by the relationship that I had lost sight of ME. When I finally decided to leave the relationship, I knew it was time to stop apologizing for loving myself and refocus on doing all things through Christ who gives me strength. I knew I never would apologize again for being me and I thank God that I have never turned back.

The Beginning

Have you ever had enough, or ever wondered if you should kill him to end your misery? My thoughts took me there on several occasions after years of being taken advantage of and just being used. My story begins when I was nineteen, I had just met a man seven years older and I was just blown away! How exciting and how impressionable I was back then. When I met him, I had only been dating for two years because my father had not approved of me dating until I turned seventeen. I really did not have much experience. At first,

Friends and Relationships

my boyfriends were mostly inexperienced adolescent guys; they had very little experience dating and so did I. Then I met this older guy and I began an entirely new experience with men. He took me downtown to very expensive restaurants, he made sure that my hair was maintained and he even purchased my clothing. In this newfound love, little did I know that I was a secret, because I found out later that there was a girlfriend. I never saw her but I knew she had to exist. At nineteen, I thought I had something very special. Unfortunately, things were not what they appeared to be. Please realize that you do not have much of a relationship when you cannot meet the family, when you cannot have a home number and when you cannot come over at all.

Well, back to the story. My beau was a professional dancer and I am not talking about hip-hop dance. The year was 1988 and he was twenty-six, he was into ballet, modern and jazz dance. He worked with a professional studio that was affiliated with Ms. Katherine Dunham. I was so impressed with his lifestyle; he had his own business and drove a nice car. However, I should have known something was up when he took me to a nice condo one day and I stayed in one of the bedrooms all day! Looking back, I have to wonder why I would agree to such treatment. But, I did not question it because what he had shown me up until that point seemed contrary to him keeping me stuck in a bedroom all day. Yet, it was not long after that I began to wonder about certain other things. I started to believe that I might be the "secret" because when he received phone calls he would immediately leave to take the call in another room. But then I thought, "Well I haven't known him that long…so, so what if he still has friends."

As time went on, the gifts were great and the wining and dining was blowing my mind. I thought how I could be so lucky to have met him because all the guys my age acted as if they were twelve. He taught many new things like how to stand straight and walk with poise; he even gave me pointers on how to interview professionally. One day he sat me down and went over questions that an interviewer would ask and he gave me the answers. Later, I went on an interview at a financial institution and got the job. I was so excited and grateful because I had never met anyone so intelligent. I ended up putting him so high on a pedestal that for a long time I was unwilling to let him come down; yet that would change.

Get a clue!

Things began to get even stranger. One evening he picked me up and at the end of the visit, he was supposed to take me home but he told me that his car had been stolen. I also would find out that the place I thought was his was actually his parents. That man was sneaking me into his parents' house and looking back I realized that except for bathroom breaks, I had to stay in his bedroom whenever I visited. The deception about his living arrangement was strike one. Only a young, inexperienced chick would have allowed this ill-treatment but I fit the profile. Sadly, I was a living example of how many young girls are manipulated and taken advantage of by older men that prey on them.

Back to the car situation, I heard him on the phone making a report with the police or so I thought. Later, I learned that this phone call was phony; he was making calls trying to find a ride to get me home. At the time, I actually felt bad for him—my handsome, intelligent and debonair guy with caramel-colored skin, a nice grade of hair, big eyes, beautiful skin, full lips and straight white teeth. He thought he was so fine that he actually brushed his eyebrows and his eyelashes; he was truly what we call a pretty boy. He actually complained that his eyelashes were too long and that they would get in his eyes... imagine that! At the end of the day, he was able to borrow his brother's car to take me home. Ladies, for weeks I would ask him if the police had found his car and his answer was always no. Guess what... his car was not stolen, it had been repossessed, strike two!

Just Blind

By the time I turned twenty I was still dating him, hoping that one day he would be my husband. A year had gone by and I continued to discover things that were just too weird to let slide. Over time I realized a good purpose for dating is to

Unapologetically Woman

look for clues to help one determine whether or not their mate is truly husband material. Be careful not to marry during the early infatuation period because usually your head is so far in the clouds that you seldom see things clearly. The clouds usually represent material things, lustful things, and anything that just feels good to you.

During this period of infatuation, I began to observe a problematic pattern—I could never find him on Friday nights or Saturday mornings. Yet, randomly on Saturday afternoons, he would call and ask me out. Generally, it would end up being late evenings when he would finally take me out on Saturdays or Sundays. Although I was fascinated to be dating an older guy, I was not the fool he expected me to be; the late night dating was unusual to me. Besides, my father had already warned me that he believed my boyfriend was married or had another woman. Nevertheless, I still did not believe he was married. My Dad advised me not to let him pick me up for late dates because it looked bad and it made my dad suspicious of him. Well I thought as long as he made time for me then it did not matter what time he picked me up.

I eventually learned that long before people began talking about the "bootie call," my father knew about these promiscuous behaviors of men. He was old school but I started listening because I knew this man was older and I was young and inexperienced. He probably thought I was just a young idiot, but all the while, I was becoming more suspicious and beginning to put the pieces together.

All Grown Up Now

I was close to turning twenty-one and looking forward to getting my first apartment. He had finally moved out of his parents' home. At once, I began to be hopeful and I thought that since he finally had his own place he might spend more time with me. However, it never happened, since I was seeing him only periodically, I began to grow apart from him. He would go days and then weeks without even calling. So what did I do… I bounced! I did not officially break up with him but in my mind it was all over. I started to develop my own group of friends that I liked to go out with for fun. Because I loved dancing, my friends and I would frequent dance clubs at least three or four times a week. During that time, a friend introduced me to a new young man who was a singer, sweet, attentive, and only twenty-one. The only problem was that he was from California. However I was overjoyed at the possibility that he would consider relocating to Illinois with his family.

As time went on, "we fell in like" and I started dating him regularly. Several weeks later, I still had not heard from my so-called man, the older guy. As far as I was concerned, I had a new male friend and the older man was fading from my memory. Then my mother informed me that my ex had begun calling my home again. Truthfully, I did not care about the older man anymore; I was young, working, and having fun with my friends. My mentality was very much like a child so absorbed with play that he/she forgets to go to the restroom--I could care less that he had decided to start calling again. My thoughts were, just keep on dating whomever you have been seeing because I'm kicking it with someone new.

I am In Trouble

One Saturday night, I was at home preparing to go out when suddenly there was a knock on the door...it was him! Oh no, I thought, it cannot be him or at least I did not want it to be because I am going out! I answered the door and there he was with his sad self and he wanted to know "what was going on." I opted not to tell him anything. Now remember, I had not heard from him or seen him in weeks why would I automatically feel as though I had to answer to someone with whom I had become so disconnected with. He wanted to know where I was going, so I told him I was going to a party with friends. He was so persistent and possessive, for an entire hour, he was berating and questioning, demanding that he go with me. I grew more desperate by the minute because I was already late meeting my friends. This man was driving me nuts so I did something very dumb...I did not want to hurt him so I tried to convince him that he could come along. I knew if I took him to my friend's home, they would not be

Friends and Relationships

there because we were meeting somewhere else. That way I could pretend that they left me and then he would go home.

Now keep in mind, I was just a twenty year old naïve youngster and I don't even understand why I decided to do things the complex way. I really do not know why I continued the charade, but I took him to my friend's home. A part of me was also trying to prove that there was no one else for him to be jealous of, but I was young and not thinking. Come to think of it, why was I trying to prove anything! Also, did I mention that he was crying? He was begging and pleading to be with me that night and that is why I ended up doing the extreme things. I wanted to prove to him that there was nothing to be jealous of and that he could go home without worry. This way I would be able to go on to meet up with my friends and my new male friend free and clear.

The elaborate charade continues and while over at the home of my new friend's parents, he was trying to put his hand on my knee and his arm around me to see if he would get a reaction. It was almost as if he knew I was deceiving him; he was an older guy so he might have known I was trying to play him. Meanwhile, my new boyfriend's little brother and sister were wondering what was going on between us because they knew I was dating their brother. What had I gotten myself into with this man! After my friend's mother confirmed everyone was gone then we left. Outside as we were leaving, I ran into my new friend's older brother; it was so awkward. I introduced my old boyfriend as "my friend" him being the possessive man that he was; he promptly corrected me and declared he was my boyfriend. At that moment, I knew… I was all messed up.

We returned to my home, and I still had to try to convince him that I did not have anybody else in my life. I really thought I had proved something by taking him to my new boyfriend's home; but he was not even convinced, and I was fed up. Why was I trying to prove myself to somebody who had not been around anyway? I realized that I was at a disadvantage dating an older person and I felt overpowered and overwhelmed. The big finale to the evening's fiasco was that I left him, crying inside my parent's house.

When I returned, my father was trying to figure out what was going on. I told him that he would not leave and I had plans so I left him there. My father told me to get rid of him and that he was only shedding crocodile tears, i.e. he was fake. I could tell my father did not like him and he knew that when a man just disappears it is usually because of another woman or something to do with a woman.

After I finally got rid of him, I really started feeling bad about how I had treated him, so I APOLOGIZED. You are probably thinking, "Why would she do that?" I did not know what to do with myself because he made me feel like I had misinterpreted his disappearing act. We got back together and my new friend went back to California.

Enduring Repetitive Behavior

By the time I turned twenty-one, I was independent and living in my own apartment. That entire year we were "back together," my boyfriend only came over twice to visit. When we spent time together, it was mostly at his place, and the disappearing acts continued. Believe it or not, I allowed his neglectful treatment to go on for another two years. By now, I had been with him for a total of four years and a whole lot had occurred between us. After my lease was up, I moved in with him. While at his place, I was not allowed to answer the phone. He even stayed away all night leaving me alone because he claimed he needed "to be there" for a friend. As it turns out, that so-called friend ended up having his baby but I did not find that out until years later.

 At twenty-three, I decided it was time to break off our so-called relationship. I was tired of his unacceptable behavior, especially his coming home with the cars of other women and staying out all night repeatedly. His business had failed so he was jobless and yet he had the nerve to continue his behavior. Therefore, after four years, I was fed up with all his mental and emotional abuse, and would not take it any longer.

After our break-up, I eventually fell in love with another man. Although we were serious, we did not last because the entire two years we were together we were stalked by my ex who made constant harassing phone calls. He also regularly sat outside my parent's home, as well as the home of the guy I was dating. This behavior continued throughout the entire time I was with my new boyfriend, it became so uncomfortable for us, and the relationship became very strained. My new boyfriend just did not trust me and assumed that my ex was still lingering around because I wanted him to be around. Over time, our conversations about my ex led to many arguments and misunderstandings. He felt as if he was in competition all the time and he grew obsessed with having to have me around him all the time.

In Love with Love Again

For two years, my ex begged me to get back with him. He promised that he would spend more time with me and that we would get married. Eventually, his persistence paid off, he was charismatic and really knew how to dazzle me. He was so convincing and the shopping sprees he lavished me with were a treat. Compared to my other boyfriend, my ex definitely had the edge when it came to pouring on the charm and I soon found myself drawn to him. Once again, I was APOLOGIZING for leaving him. Why would I do this to myself? I guess I was hoping that his words would be true this time because I was in love with the idea of marriage. As it turns out all of his promises ended up being a lie! Today I know only the word of God to be true.

After we got back together, the next two years I spent with him were pure hell and he treated me worse than ever before. His behavior became so much worse because he could not forgive me for moving on to another relationship. See while in that relationship with the other guy I had visited him twice when he was in the hospital for two different suicide attempts, he still harbored anger towards me. Evidently, the suicide attempts were due to my leaving him, beginning a new relationship, and refusing to get back with him. He blamed me, for his desire to end his life. The same man who had barely spent time with me when we were together, who was caught in constant lies, who played disappearing acts and knew he had a baby with another woman while in a relationship with me, was now claiming that he was suicidal and in the hospital because of me. Now that I was back with him, he seized the opportunity to dog me every chance he got, revenge was alive!

Enduring Revenge

I should have had enough by now but I remained in the relationship. I thought I would be in this situation for the rest of my life because I had agreed to return to him. My mind was made up and I was not ever going to break it off with him again or allow another guy to come in between the two of us. He had me I would find receipts for items he purchased for other women. I also found ticket stubs to movies he had attended with other women. One day I broke the code to his cell phone and listened to his voicemails; wow did the Red Sea open when I heard some of those voicemails! It is not worth repeating what I heard but the messages were not a surprise. Finally, I had proof that it was more than just one woman. Vengeance was truly in action and he was taking me through hell on purpose. It was so bad that one time he cheated while we were in Alabama at his family reunion. At the reunion he kept urging me to go out with his sisters; I could not figure out why he wanted me to go with them so desperately. In fact, we almost got into an argument because he was demanding that I leave from being with him to go out with his sisters. Do you know that he seized that opportunity to go out with another woman! He was gone all that night and the next morning; we were out of town and he was still behaving in a blatant and spiteful way. I later discovered what he was up to after finding photos of the woman he was with on that very trip.

Another incident occurred after we went to lunch and an early show. He had seemed pretty eager to get rid of me and abruptly suggested that I visit my parents. When he asked me for money, I hesitated because I wondered if he were spending it on other women. When I refused to give him the mon-

Friends and Relationships

ey, we argued, he jumped in his car and drove off in a huff. I tried to follow him but he noticed my trail and dodged me…you will never believe what happened next: I went to my parents' house where I had left a list of phone numbers and addresses that I found by going through his voicemails. After reviewing the addresses, I chose one address in the immediate area and went there to look for him. Sure enough, his red mustang GT was parked out front. At that precise moment, I felt like killing him. I knocked on the door and an older woman answered, so I asked for him. When he came to the door, I snapped. I spoke to the young lady he was visiting with respect and found out that she was very young and had not known him that long. If he was seven years older than I was, he had to be twelve years older than her. Later when he got in his car, I tried to run him off the road, by now things had gotten dangerous. Sometime later, things calmed down and we discussed the incident…once again, I accepted the lie that he was sorry and we continued in this relationship.

Last but not least, I made a new discovery during my investigation through his phone; I found out that he was getting into a serious relationship with one particular woman. I had several conversations with her and discovered that he was playing us both. He told her lies about me, and lied about the relationship that we had. What hurt me the most was that he did not respect me enough to give me any explanation at all when I confronted him about his cheating. Nevertheless, he had the nerve to tell her stories about me, and he felt he did not owe me anything since I had hurt him; this was the final strike! When I saw how he had turned against me, all I could do was turn to God at that point. There was nothing my best friend, my father or anyone else could have said to me to make me feel better. See I could not leave by my own will because the competition with her and the fear of her winning became more of the issue than me seeing him continue a relationship with her. I continued to live with this man and I refused to "lose" him to her.

Desperate for Separation

One night I fell to my knees crying out to God in desperation for him to help me to leave the bondage of that relationship; a soul tie that only God could break. I tried to have that last talk with him and he said the most devastating thing to me of all times; He said, "It hurts to be with you and it hurts to be without you." What exactly he meant I would never know, but I needed the confidence in God that I would be all right if I left him for good. Then I also needed the boldness of God to get it done. One night out of nowhere, I got up and called the taxi, packed all my clothes and never turned around. God set it up so that he did not even try to resist my leaving. He did not say a word to me as I packed and I am sure he thought that this was what he wanted as well. I was finally desperate enough to leave that unhealthy relationship.

Friends and Relationships

In addition, when I finally left him, my relationship with God was restored and I survived.

Can you believe after all that happened between us, this man thought that I would still return to him? He was like the enemy-- never resting until he breaks or devours you. For an entire year, he would not give up but called my job and my home insistently. Some phone calls I would take and others I would deny. My father would give me messages that he had called on some weekends, but I had resolved within myself to move on. He would ask me out but I did not respond because it was as if he was throwing out bait to see if I would bite. I liked that he was suffering, for years I had been intrigued with his pursuit but now it did not appeal to me at all. Finally, God removed the desire to be with him from my soul completely.

A Surprise!

The next time he was able to reach me, I was happily married and he cried in disbelief. He wondered why I would marry someone else. I replied without apology, someone else had found me and discovered my value; I had finally broken free from our vicious make-up and break-up cycle. Through my relationship with Jesus Christ, I had begun loving myself, regaining my self-respect, and getting stronger. It did not matter anymore that he cried and asked questions because I was in a new frame of mind and I no longer felt the need to apologize—uh, uh, not this time! I was stronger and finally free… I discovered that I can do all things through Christ who strengthens me. (Philippians 4:13)

Foreword for Desiree M. Fleming

Women of integrity carry a lot on their shoulders today. Many times, forgetting about themselves women of integrity use their strengths to help others. Unyielding selflessness can leave many burned out.

Unapologetically Woman is a book of testimonials by women sharing their inner strengths—strengths that lay silently within and which are only activated when in dire need or when you find yourself pushed up against a wall. Desiree Fleming encourages women to wake up, get over it, and move on. Her message to women specifically is to wake up the sleeping giant within, finally pat yourself on the back, and say, "I owe no man an apology for I am somebody."

In 2 Kings 7:3, the scripture says, *Why sit we here until we die? Let us try something now (KJV)*. When I think of the writings of Desiree Fleming, I think of a strong woman who has been there. She lets you know you do not have time to let depression, oppression, and low esteem enter into your world. You cannot give up on life because you have had a detour. Shake yourself off and stand up for "you don't owe anybody anything." To put it another way, you are beautiful and wonderfully made; be confident in whatever decisions you make so that you do not and will not apologize.

Bishop Linda C. Shearrill
International Deliverance Outreach Ministries

Unapologetically Woman, a woman who lives without regrets or excuses, is exactly who Desiree Fleming has become. As a fellow author, I urge readers to embrace the life changing words written by Desiree. Knowing Desiree for as long as I have, I know she has truly gone deep inside of herself to give you the truth behind why she is Unapologetically Woman. I have had the opportunity to mentor and pastor Desiree, for more than ten years. Her life has had many ups and downs, losses and disappointments, but never has she allowed the circumstances of her life to offer failure as an option. This book is a must for any woman whether she's a married, single or divorced, stay at home mom, a president of a company or a woman struggling in poverty. I believe that as you read this book you will find that you will find the strength to reach your fullest potential and wildest dreams without apologies or regrets.

Rev. Dr. Alexander Gee Jr.
Senior Pastor
Fountain of Life Ministries

Desiree M. Fleming

Desiree is a wife, mother, daughter, sister, Empowerment Coach, business owner, friend, and one of the most empowering, influential women in the Midwest. The chief Editor of EJF Publishing & Printing, she is the author of a riveting, and inspirational novel of healing and hope, "Where Could I Take My Shame?" Her novel offers encouragement to anyone who has suffered from sexual, mental, or physical abuse. Desiree is also the Chief Editor of the "Unapologetically Woman" project.

Desiree holds a BA in Urban Ministry. She has shared her writings via the internet, newsletters, and other publications, garnering numerous requests for more works of her powerful words. She is selfless when it comes to empowering others to dream bigger than a dream, to live larger than life, and to make it happen no matter what. Married to Pastor Jeremiah Fleming, Desiree has two children, Ronald (Brittney) and E'lisa, raising one niece, Briana and three nephews, Jamaal, Joshua and Charles, and also blessed with one granddaughter, Kyleigh.

Friendship at its Purest
By Desiree Fleming

Identity Crisis

After I gave birth to my second child, my eyes finally opened to the TRUTH about my friendships and life. Finding me has not been an easy feat. I began to recognize how demanding, dominating, and controlling many of my friendships were and I could hardly believe my predicament. Although I was actually saying words, I realized I was failing to communicate effectively what was in my heart because of my low self-esteem and feelings of worthlessness. Outwardly, I appeared to have it going on, but inwardly the demons of fear and low self-esteem taunted me with negative thoughts—"Play it safe," "What you're saying isn't that important," and "They really aren't interested in your opinion."

I did not realize that people usually can tell when you are struggling with low self-esteem. Low self-esteem is not really hidden like we think. In fact, low self-esteem broadcasts messages like "I'm nothing, "I wish I was dead," and "I feel incompetent." Haunted by my inadequacies, I ended up conforming to the expectations of others. Instead of blazing my own trail, I was lurking in the shadows of others trying to fulfill a purpose other than my own. Truthfully, I had lost track

Friends and Relationships

of my voice and identity and did not even recognize the person I had become. Sometimes when we do not value ourselves we often settle for less, be it employment, lifestyles, friends or lovers. It is not until we value who we are that we can truly enjoy friendship at its purest.

Friendships

In my life, I have had many friendships; some were healthier than others were. Since learning what healthy friendships truly look like, I would like to share some ways you can evaluate the quality of your current and future friendships to determine if they are indeed healthy. We know that some friendships create difficulties, but healthy friendships can be very rewarding. My goal is to encourage you to identify and pursue those friendships that will nurture and build you up, instead of those that tear you down.

During my childhood, I had several friends in my neighborhood and in my childish way I thought I understood true friendship. In our neighborhood, we had unspoken codes to determine whether a person was a true friend. For example, one had a "true friendship" when the person was able to keep your secrets, when you made up quickly after a disagreement, when you helped another if a fight broke out, or when you hung out and played together all the time. Actually, that unspoken code of friendship was not too far off from reality. These basic codes are really still needed for great friendships to work today.

Looking back, I realize there were several ways I subscribed to that unspoken code; I also see how I failed. One area of particular difficulty was finding models of healthy, balanced friendships with females in my life. When I watched women "dog out" one another, lie and use deceit or manipulation in the name of friendship, I was appalled. How could women who laughed with each another and hung out together treat each other that way? Without being fully aware of it, I developed distrust toward other women. Therefore, growing into womanhood I thought that to fit in, I needed to be fake.

As a teenager, I always preferred talking to guys and so I ended up with more guy friends than girl friends because it just seemed more manageable. I did not have to deal with all the gossip and jealousy issues that girls evoked. One day I suddenly realized that I had cut off almost all my friendships with girls. I had no girls to discuss my common female problems with or share any of my aspirations.

When I got married at the tender age of nineteen, I brought all my insecurities about female friendships right in my new marriage. I had little direction, limited education, no experience, no employment and no one to call a friend. Ladies, my husband Jeremiah was in for the ride of his life. I was an

Friends and Relationships

insecure young single mother who desired to spend all of my time with my new husband because I was absolutely, friendless! Everywhere he went, I was there with him and this went on for years. It felt so much easier to be with my husband than to hang out with other women. However, as much as I adored being with my husband, my husband could never fill the need for positive, healthy friendships with other women.

Trust issues surfacing

I soon realized that I needed to be more open to developing female friendships. Still, it has not been easy to establish and maintain balanced friendships with other women. I am friendly and outgoing but inwardly the little girl in me remembers the scarcity of real, authentic relationships with girls. Trust issues were at the core of my frustration because I never knew who was being real. The echoes of my mother words, "You can't trust her," reverberated in my ears; does that sound familiar? What was I to do with this information coming from my own mother? After all, she was my mentor and my reliable source for information, right. Well, that is what I thought and it did not matter who the potential friend was, I always assumed that all girls, and later women, were evil had wrong motives, and I dare not trust any of them. This underlying distrust made me distance myself from other women and limited the growth of adult friendships.

As I struggled to figure out the best way to relate to women, the Lord began healing me of my fears and trust issues. Gradually, I began to open my heart to the possibility of having what I could call true friendships: wholesome, authentic, and healthy. In the process of healing, I have developed the following characteristics of "unhealthy friendships:"

You know you are in an unhealthy friendship when . . .

1. Your friend tries to change who you are
2. Someone is always controlling your time and tracking your movements
3. Someone is speaking death to you and undermining your marriage
4. You find yourself more concerned about what someone else thinks about you rather than what the Word of God or your husband says about you
5. You let their opinions undercut your self-perception
6. You are uncomfortable seeing them
7. You fear speaking to the person on the phone, so you avoid calling—instead you text them or leave voicemails
8. The issues at hand are always about them and hardly ever about you
9. You find yourself always giving and never receiving, except for receiving bad advice
10. You become overly possessive of the other person, or vice versa

Friends and Relationships

11. You find yourself always depending on them for "the answer"
12. You start neglecting home to do things for them
13. You cannot have a normal day without talking to them
14. You find yourself constantly complaining about the unhealthy nature of your relationship, but remain connected regardless

Keeping these characteristics in mind, I took a hard look at my relationships and realized that I needed a healthier quality to my current friendships. How could I find women who would be true friends, "for real"? I know now that my struggle was not unique; many women are struggling to maintain healthy relationships due to past issues, insecurity, low self-esteem, and trust factors among other things. Whether at school, in the work place, at church, in community, or in immediate family, I have found that other women struggle in the pursuit for true friendship daily just as I was struggling.

"Finding Me"

I discussed briefly the friendships of childhood, now I will fast forward to a time in adulthood when I began searching to find myself. Right before the birth of my second child a few years ago, I started something new. I started valuing and guarding my space and my time; I would always make time to talk on the phone with my friends. Of course, after my baby was born I did not have the same availability so I needed to make a drastic change to manage my schedule. There had to be a change in my schedule so that the majority of my attention, affection, and nurture could be shifted to my newborn daughter. This was a critical time in my child's life and I finally had to come to my senses. For example, I needed to breastfeed my baby and stop trying to cater to the whims of friends. Now, do not get me wrong, this was not an easy or smooth transition. I have found that most changes come with opposition and challenges, and having a new baby was no different. When you have spent most of your life trying to please people, it is always hard to make a change. When people are accustomed to you acting one way, it is not easy for them to adjust to your new behavior. Only those who love you and are not threatened by your growth or success are able to support you through whatever life transition you may encounter.

Eventually, it no longer mattered anymore what people thought or expected from me. Making a change in my nature and dependency on others was a matter of life and death, and trust me I was not prepared to die. I did not want to be that same "little girl" in my friendships any longer. I wanted to be the woman I am unapologetically, with no excuses or regrets. As a result, I found myself avoiding phone calls, text messages, and emails so I did not have to hear or read about some-

Friends and Relationships

one's disappointment or frustration if I were not available for them. Whew, talk about feeling as if you are in bondage! At times, I felt stuck as if I was a ten-year-old girl, trying to fit into an adult's world.

Ladies, remember it will always cost you something to go to the next level in your life. The cost just might be that "unhealthy friendship" you cling to but, please do not be fearful of or resist going on to the next level. Going on to that next level for me meant dealing with one friendship in particular that was far too demanding and unhealthy. I had a friend who always wanted me to devote all of my attention to her whenever we were on the phone. Now, keep in mind I was a married woman, with a young teenage son, and I was a busy business owner. In my desire to please this friend, I would literally tell my husband and son, "I will talk to you when I get off the phone." I would hush them, putting a finger up to signal them to be quiet… and soon this became a regular habit. It was as if my marriage and family life came to a complete stop whenever this particular friend would call. When I look back on that time in my life, I was like a prisoner in that friendship, and dragged my family right in the cell with me. At times, I cannot believe how long I allowed myself to be enslaved by this ridiculous behavior.

Furthermore, there were times when this friend treated me as if I were invisible during conversations with other women. I would feel so small, I would end up slumped in my seat and this so-called friend would speak right past me as if I were not even sitting there. She acted as if I could not comprehend what was going on in the conversation. I am not sure if it were because she had obtained her college degree and therefore felt better than me, or if it was just because of my own insecurity about not having a degree myself. On the other hand, maybe she was masking her own insecurities by presenting herself as superior. Whatever the reason, she always seemed to be indirectly putting me down, like when she shared information about her employment or accomplishments, she would always direct it toward our mutual friends, who had also graduated from college. For years, I kept my mouth shut allowing what seemed like slights jabs to my character but it eventually began to take a toll mentally. For some reason I felt as if I was constantly being subjected to mental abuse. A few times, she off-handedly quipped, "Desiree, I forget at times you didn't graduate from college." Was that supposed to be an insult or compliment, I was not sure because I was so beaten down that it was difficult to tell her intentions. Still, I wondered about true relevance of that comment in our current conversation.

As time progressed, I found that I would always be angry whenever I left a lunch or an outing where she was involved because her behavior and actions were so demeaning and disrespectful. Enduring her snobbish behavior reminded me of my frustration in dropping out of high school when I did not

Friends and Relationships

have any solid plans for my life. Experiencing not having friends and not wanting to abandon my current friendships, I just dealt with her intellectual insults for years. I was almost forty years old before I began to critically evaluate all my relationships, including this one. Little by little, I began reclaiming my life and the voice I had relinquished to be accepted by others. For the first time, I began to discover who I really was and see myself as God sees me. Finally, what God was saying to me about my life mattered the most, not what others had to say. I decided I no longer needed to allow feelings of inadequacy and self-defeat to keep me entangled in unfruitful friendships. I realized that I could bless my friends by allowing them to connect with me as a Christian, and as a woman of value and courage.

Besides, being myself and not conforming to the mold others constructed for me, I could offer my friends the benefit of pure friendship—respect, trust, and love.

If It Doesn't Fit, Don't Force It

Armed with my newfound mentality, I knew it was time to be released from certain unhealthy relationships. Although, as a friend I grew to care more for my friends, I could not be held hostage by other's expectations any longer; the unhealthy friendships had to be severed. Seeking greater things in life, I was ready to sacrifice the small and trivial to get to where I needed to be. I re-evaluated all my relationships that were not working for me, and even if people were not pure evil or out to sabotage me, it was my time to move on. I figured if the relationship "did not fit, don't force it!"

In my life, I probably had only one true friendship where I was free to be myself. In the healthy relationship, I did not have to cheer all of her choices, or do everything she did to make it work. Our relationship was built on "me being me" and "her being her." Although we did not talk much, whenever we did it was always encouraging, motivating, and healthy. I never felt like she was trying to destroy my life or shape me into a mini version of her; she gave me room to be me, as I did her. I am so grateful that our friendship has no strings attached, and that I am able to trust in her as a true friend!

Today, I no longer live by the definition of others, their opinions, and their thoughts or ideas of me. No longer do I make apologies for my accomplishments, successes, or inadequacies to maintain friendships. Ladies, in my quest for becoming "Unapologetically Woman," I had to learn to love and accept the person God created me to be.

Friends and Relationships

I am who I am for I have sacrificed all those fears and anxieties that held me in bondage so that my daughter can have a positive role model. I want her to know how to love herself without regrets or restrictions. I am unapologetically woman and I love being me!

Section Three
Who's That Woman in the Mirror?

Foreword for Kim Miller

I had often heard about Kim Miller and her women's ministry over the years. I had the pleasure of finally meeting her at the National Women's Forum in 2009. We learned that we were both Mary Kay consultants who had chosen to exemplify the golden rule—prefer your sister over yourself. While working beside each other, we learned that we were actually on the same national team, with the same national director—kindred spirits indeed!

I admired the pretty, petite, but elegant woman of God. She exemplified the quiet reserve fit for a queen. She invited me to attend her Women of Valor's annual conference. I was elated to do so. I noticed the grace and poise she exemplified as she led the women in worship, introduced the speakers, and candidly shared her life's journey. Kim spoke from her soul and touched the lives of her women. It was powerful to see a First Lady mingle so well with her women. The event was exceptional and fun as the ladies also took a boat ride on Lake Michigan—no ordinary weekend.

I enjoyed reading Lady K's chapter on how her life evolved from childhood as she sought to answer the question… "Who Am I?"

Learning the answer to this question leads a woman to her destiny and a life without apologies or compromise. In this chapter, I like many other women, will learn who Lady Kim Miller really is...fascinating, mysterious, nurturing and confident. Her story demonstrates her strength. She is unashamed of her past, yet excited about her future. We are too!

L. Renee Richardson
Founder & CEO,
Women of Vision & Destiny, Inc.

Kim W. Miller

Kim is the Director of the Women of Valor, Inc., of Life Christian Center International in Bellwood, Illinois. She is also the CEO and President of Purposed by Design Consulting and an Independent Beauty Consultant with Mary Kay Corporation. Born, raised, and educated in Chicago, Illinois Kim has three sisters, Karen, Gabrielle, and Angela. Kim graduated from Jones Commercial High School in 1976 before attending college part time.

Kim has always had the aspiration and mindset to be a leader. She has exhibited those skills time and time again in various administrative roles. She has worked for The Quaker Oats Company, a subsidiary of PepsiCo a Fortune 500 Corporation as well as for the Village of Bellwood.

Currently, Kim is a student with University of Phoenix. She is married to Bishop Miller and is the First Lady of Life Christian Center International, located in Bellwood, Illinois. She has four children and is a contributing author with EJF Publishing and Printing, Inc.

Who Am I?
By Kim W. Miller

Have you ever found yourself wondering, "Who am I?" I know I have pondered this question often. After many years of searching, falling down, and getting back up again, I believe I have found the answer. It has certainly been a long journey of self-discovery, but I finally know who I am and who I was created to be.

On November 17, 1958 I entered the world at Cook County Hospital in Chicago, Illinois. The first daughter of Eunice A. Leak and Will Vaughn Dye, my parents named me Kim. At the time, I had no clue what was ahead of me and never imagined what the world had in store or that I was born for any particular purpose.

Our family lived on the southeast Side of Chicago at 63rd and University. For my first few years, I was raised there with my sister, Karen, who was born March 24, 1961. One of my early memories is our move to one of the newly built projects of the Chicago Housing Authority system. I was five then and living with my mother, my stepfather, Arthur Jefferson, and my sister. At five years old, I did not totally understand what a true treasure it was to live with both parents and have a complete family. All I knew at that time was family!

I enjoyed my childhood, from what I can remember—our family trips down South to Mississippi, getting sick from my travels, my Mom giving me her homemade remedy of boiled rice-water, having birthday parties, getting dressed up and yes, taking plenty of pictures! I was living a carefree life and I was totally clueless of the special calling dwelling in me. Still, a question was beginning to form deep within my soul: "Who Am I?"

I remember being a semi-active child with an inward desire to please everyone. That tendency continued into my adult life and I did not realize this attribute was actually part of my nature. I found myself wanting to please others, but I still had a tugging on the inside to unlock the doors of my curiosity to self-discovery. Without even realizing it, my journey to becoming an unapologetic woman had already begun.

It began with the fearless attitude of a child dreaming of who she wants to be when she grows up. It was so wonderful to be young and full of dreams and goals, with no hindrances or limitations about the choices I wanted and intended to make. But then somewhere during my journey, fear came to steal every fiber of ambition, aspiration, and dream. It caused me to do a double take and or re-think the ideas that came to me in a night dream. Fear caused me to step back from those creative and inspired moments that would catapult me right into my God-given purpose and destiny if I had only moved upon them immediately. In Jeremiah 29:11 the Word of the Lord states: "For I know the plans I have for you," declares the LORD, "plans to prosper you and not to harm you, plans to give you hope and a future "(NIV Version). Fear came to rob me of my future.

During my formative years, my gifts and talents were beginning to surface, but neither my family nor I clearly recognized them. Although God-given seeds were planted deeply within my spirit, I often found myself asking the question "Who Am I?" throughout my high school, college and adult life. I was living at home and facing real–life challenges. Taking on adult responsibilities at an early age, I found my place of security and safety in my relationship with God. My security blanket became Psalms 91:1-2: "He who dwells in the secret place of the most High, shall abide under the shadow of the Almighty. I will say of the Lord He is my refuge and my fortress" (NKJV). Thankfully, my Mom accepted Christ into her life while I was very young, and she led me to the one that would undoubtedly shine the light on who I really am!

Growing up, peer pressure often led me down wrong pathways. Encouraged to bow to the false identities at that stage of life, I heard deceptive voices trying to convince me "that's who you are" and "that's who you should be." Sometimes, it was the challenge to "assume that look;" "take on that attitude," or "accept that way of life." "Do it quickly and do it now because you know you can't go through life not knowing who you are even if it may cost you your life!" These masked identities sought to grab hold of the confidence embedded within in my soul from birth and sabotage the creative, productive human being that God intended me to be; they tried to shake me loose from every purpose I was intended to fulfill.

To discover who I am, I had to honestly come to grips with my likes and dislikes. I had to take a good look at what I did not like about me and find out what I did like. All the while, the question remained and still lingering in my soul was "Who Am I?" Walking down the road of enlightenment, I reflected on my many choices and acknowledged my mistakes. I thought to myself, "If I could only do it over again, things surely would be different! I would be more confident and knowledgeable in declaring and staking claim on my position in life."

After years of searching, I am now aware of who I am and who I was created to be! I am Unapologetically Woman! I know that I am not perfect; I am a woman tall in spirit but short in stature. I am ready to put the past behind me and accelerate into my future! I am a curvaceous woman, not by choice but genetics. Although for many years in my life, I was comparing myself to everyone else hoping to change the way I looked, I finally recognized the tremendous amount of talent, inspiration, wisdom, and knowledge I have to offer this world. As I have grown older and wiser, I now understand that God made me, fearfully and wonderfully. I am who I am because that is just what God planned. Truly, I am a design original!

Having lived most of my life with an inferiority complex, I am so glad I overcame that negative mindset. Embracing my worth as a woman and discovering my spiritual identity have been powerful assets. Now, I know that I am more than a conqueror! I recognize that ". . . in all these things we are more than conquerors through Him who loved us" (Romans 8:37 NKJV).

There is a song that says, "I'm Every Woman, It's all in Me;" I am not so sure about this concept. For me, I am learning to stand on God's Word alone, for myself. I know I have been equipped to handle every challenge that I face. With the strength of the powerful life-giving word of God, I can do all things. I am a product of faith-filled words blowing over the sometimes dead, listless branches of my existence transforming me into an ever-blossoming tree! I offer no excuses for who I am. I am that unapologetic woman of integrity and strength. I may or may not be what you expect, but I definitely will be what my Creator intended for me to be! God

Who's That Woman in the Mirror?

did not intend for me to be anyone else but me and I have to answer to Him for every ounce of talent He has placed within me. I have the opportunity to touch each human being I encounter with the talents God has given me. I will not compromise my state of well-being or apologize for being who God says I am!

I am a woman living in a defining moment for I am becoming history in the making for generations to come. This is the moment I have been purposed for and destined to unite with since the beginning of my time. I cannot and will not apologize for who I am. I am a thinker, a writer, a woman of praise, and a giver of worship and adoration to my Lord and King. My past has helped me to rise to this elevating passion and I will never allow it to be buried in my mind or in the pages of the grave. My expressions and illumination of thought shall be exposed to the many hearts that are just waiting to know for certain that none of us ever has to fear, fret, fail or faint!

Today I am calling out to everyone who is asking the question "Who Am I?" Come out of the dark hidden corners of self-created caves, the web of mind games, the overpopulated fear zones, and the rundown ruins of "I don't know who I really am" or "what I was put on this earth for" stances we create to protect ourselves. I came out and finally discovered who I am and whose I am. I am a woman formed from the rib of man – a daughter, wife, mother, pastor's wife, encourager, writer, friend, royal priest, more than a conqueror, a worshipper, fearless warrior, authoritative and anointed spokesperson, and a design original....I AM KIM....and I am Unapologetically Woman!

Lady K

Foreword for Angela Morgan

There are many women who have decided to allow the things they have experienced define them. They see themselves as what they have encountered which oftentimes puts them in a place of victimization. As a result, they are frozen in the role of victim as opposed to that of victor. This type of rationalization cripples and may even paralyze them to the point that they no longer desire or even think they have worth or real purpose.

In this chapter, Angela offers an authentic display of transparency. This overcoming woman communicates a message that is indeed vital and pivotal in this season. She openly displays some of her most devastating trials that later became triumphs. Through Angela, we see what trusting the Lord can truly accomplish. May the blessings of God Almighty be upon this great wife, mother, grandmother, great writer, and Proverbs 31 woman. May every reader be uplifted and inspired that she too can be a Comeback Queen!

Apostle R. L. Morgan
Radical End Time Ministries International, Inc.

Angela Morgan

Angela is a woman of great compassion who has dedicated nearly half of her life to bringing healing to hurting women of all ages. She is the founder of Radical End Time Handmaidens, a ministry designed to help women overcome the history of their pasts and equip them in fulfilling their destinies. She provides prayer, intervention, and accountability as tools to rebuild lives.

Angela serves alongside her husband as Co-Pastor of Radical End Time Ministries International, Inc., in Chicago, Illinois. She has written several plays, skits and poetry. Angela and her husband, Renaldo, have three children and two grandchildren.

THE QUEEN OF COMEBACK
By Angela Denise Morgan

Defining Moments: Taking It All In

It is so easy to be mad at God and the world, who better to blame than God when tragedy strikes. Why did He allow it to happen? Putting God on trial seems so much easier than the reality: bad things do happen to good people. Through it all, I have learned that God is faithful regardless. The devil meant it for my bad, but God meant it for my good.

As I reflect back over my life, I am inundated with memories some good and some bad. Oftentimes my struggles were both so unbelievable and unbearable that I saw no light at the end of the tunnel. The greatest lesson I have learned through my life's experiences is that everything that should have killed my hopes, my dreams, and me has only made me stronger. Somehow, through my pain, a strong determination to survive was guiding me and pushing me towards my healing and I began to understand fully who I am. Who am I today? I am The Queen of Comeback. I offer no regrets and no excuses for who I am, for I am Undoubtedly, Unequivocally, Unashamedly…Unapologetically Woman!

Who's That Woman in the Mirror?

It is my prayer that this chapter will inspire you to push past your issues and help you to love yourself. The most important thing in life is not about how you start but it is all about how you finish. Do not live your life in regret because of past failures. Your life may have been shattered by dysfunction, but you are not alone. I have come to realize that dysfunction happens even in functional families and you can still make it despite what you have gone through.

 If you are a woman who has suffered abuse of any kind (mental, physical, psychological, sexual or verbal), I encourage you to take the necessary steps to regain back control of your life. You may have lost everything you had; been addicted to alcohol and/or drugs; faced a life-threatening event; suffered betrayal; loss of a child, spouse, parent or sibling; had thoughts of committing suicide or you may have even been addicted to the wrong types of men. No matter what category you fall in, you must endeavor to find the champion within.

I believe that even before I was born, the odds were already stacked against me. I was born to a teenage mother who raised me as a single parent, grew up in the projects on the south side of Chicago and had a father who was not a consistent figure in my life. I witnessed many unhealthy and violent relationships as well. Because of my environment, I was given a great deal of responsibility so early on that it caused me to mature too fast. These factors alone placed me at a higher risk to become a product of my poor environment. God definitely had another plan because today, I am a woman whose painful journey has led me to discover both healing and wholeness. I am living out my purpose, which is to minister to hurting women regardless of age, background, race or religion.

There are defining moments in all of our lives where our circumstances will reveal our true character. Being molested as a young girl, delivering a stillborn son and suffering from the sudden loss of my mother, I would say were the three most defining moments in my life. How could someone who was emotionally shipwrecked and sinking very fast able to make a comeback? By taking it all in, I was forced to look at everything—the good, the bad and the ugly. There was a battle going on in my mind and I knew that I needed help badly. Beyond anything human, only the divine power of God was going to help me. In each of my defining moments, I kept hearing "it is not over, it's not over!" I had been to my lowest place and the only place left for me to go, was up; therefore I am no longer a victim, but a victor. I am so much more than what I had been through and now I finally know what Marvin Sapp means in his song, *"Never Would Have Made It"*.

Looking at my defining moments, I was able to see strength that I never knew I possessed. Growing up, you never imagine the kind of things I went through happening to you.

We are groomed early in childhood to pretend, leaving little room for reality when life does not happen the way we thought it should. I learned how to use the negative things that affected my life to help influence someone else's life in a positive way. Fitness trainers often tell you "no pain, no gain" – I found out this principle the hard way. I decided I could not allow my past to dictate my future any longer. Without God in my life, I am totally convinced that I would not be here today.

Exposed Too Early

A preacher once made a profound statement, that once a child is molested they stop growing emotionally. His revelation helped me to understand the reason why I struggled so many years after being molested; I was growing physically, but emotionally and mentally I was stunted. I was around ten and a half years of age, when the molestation occurred. I always thought my mother was too protective of me, not wanting me to go to sleepovers as my other friends were allowed to do. She was always so cautious and did not leave us with just anyone. The night my mother let her guard down and left my brother and me in the care of our uncle while they went out would prove to be a big mistake. That night would change my life forever leaving me with years of scars and insecurities. I was exposed too early to a violation of my body that would force me to come face to face with my uncle's perversion.

I was a very hard sleeper before being molested, but after that night, I began waking up at the slightest of noise. I would jump at the sound of someone in my room, often tying myself up in bed sheets to protect myself in case someone came in to touch me. Being exposed too early to sex of any kind can leave you traumatized and confused for years. It would take many years before I would ever again feel safe enough to just fall asleep. Innocence as I once knew it to be, would forever be gone.

I was blessed with a husband who was able to handle having his wife jumping up terrified whenever he came into our bedroom at night while I slept. One night in particular, I jumped up out of my sleep with both hands pointed as if I had a gun and I was making noises as if I was shooting at him. He knew if I had a real gun, I probably would have killed him; he comforted me and apologized relentlessly for my abuse. I rationalized that the reason why I was molested was because I had developed so early and was very shapely. I felt like my body had somehow betrayed me, I blamed myself and became angry. I was angry that what happened to me was not really dealt with properly. I mean, the subject of sexual molestation is usually taboo, something families do not like to talk about. Many of our families have adopted the "no snitch rule" and thus the unnecessary abuse continues; we definitely have to change this vicious cycle.

Later, I began to suffer from anxiety attacks because I was not ready to deal with what had happened to me. Being exposed too early caused me to develop an unhealthy fear of opening up. These anxiety attacks were the scariest things I had ever experienced and they were ruling my life. I knew that God was a healer but I began to doubt Him and I thought I was going to die. My heart felt like it was going to come out of my chest and on several occasions, I was taken by ambulance to the emergency room. I wanted to ease my family's mind that I was not losing my mind but even I was not totally convinced of the fact. I developed an addiction to muscle relaxers that were prescribed to me to help with the anxiety. My husband persuaded me to throw away my pills because of the negative effects they were having on me; it was time for me to trust completely in the same Jesus that I had told so many others about.

It was not until years after I was married, that I saw an Oprah show about children who were molested that I was able to truly confront my past. Once I faced my past, I no longer needed the pills; God brought the healing that I so desperately needed and brought balance to my life. I was no longer angry with my uncle but I knew that I needed to forgive him. Remember, forgiveness is not for the one who needs forgiveness, but forgiveness is really for you. Forgiveness does not mean that you have to deny what happened. Although I cannot explain why this happened to me, I can truly say that it feels good to be better and not bitter.

My advice is to embrace the woman you are today. Don't spend the rest of your life trying to explain why you are the way God made you to be; trust me some people will never understand anyway. Write your own emancipation proclamation and begin to celebrate yourself. With all that has happened to you, your life could have been over a long time ago. You are blessed, bold and beautiful so say it until you believe it. Allow the light to shine from within and others will see that sparkle when they look into those beautiful eyes that were once stained with tears.

Almost Broken

I have had the pleasure of birthing three beautiful children without any complications but I was not prepared for what would transpire in my fourth pregnancy. Nine years after giving birth to my last child, I found out that I was pregnant. My husband and I decided not to have more children; but I have often heard that if you want to make God laugh…tell Him your plans.

One December day, an incident happened to me that I will never forget, while riding an elevator with a co-worker, there was a woman who looked a little strange staring right at me. She proceeded to ask me if I were pregnant. I got a little offended because I did not even look pregnant but I just responded by telling her that no, I must be pregnant with ministry. Right then the elevator doors opened and she followed me out of the elevator, this woman was persistent. I turned back to look at her and she told me in a confident tone, "the day that you find out you're pregnant, you will remember my face," and she just walked away. Of course, I nervously tried to laugh it off but my co-worker did not believe this was a coincidence. Two months, later I found out that I was pregnant and I remembered the woman's face just as she said I would.

During my third my month, I threatened a miscarriage and was placed on bed rest. I had an ultrasound that revealed that I had placenta previa (the placenta was detaching from my uterus) and I was told there was great concern regarding the growth of my baby. At this point, I was referred to a women's clinic specializing in high-risk pregnancy for the duration of the pregnancy. I was told after a series of ultrasounds that my baby could be severely deformed and I may want to consider abortion as an option. How could this happen to me…I did not ask for this. However, an amniocentesis later confirmed that there were no deformities—I cried, praised and thanked God.

During my last visit, the team of doctors decided it was best to take the baby in my seventh month but I needed a series of steroid shots to mature his lungs. The night before I was scheduled to go in to induced labor, I began experiencing some discomfort. When I got to the hospital that morning, I was not prepared for the news that they could not find a heartbeat; I would have to deliver the baby immediately. The pain I experienced delivering my stillborn son was beyond anything you could imagine. The morphine drip did not help; I thought I was going to die—I wanted to die.

After the delivery, I was taken back to the same floor with women who were holding their newborn babies. I felt like someone had played a cruel joke on me but my husband got in that hospital bed with me and held me for what seemed like an eternity. It took everything in me to leave that hospital without my baby for this was not how it was supposed to end. When I got home, I did not want to leave my home, I did not want to even out of the bed. It seemed as if I could hear a baby crying, and I cried all the time. All I wanted to do was sleep and even though I had the best support system in the world, it did not stop me from spiraling downward.

I remember my mother calling to check on me every day trying to get me out of the house. I had been in the house for so long that once I got out, I started having feelings of anxiety. The look that I saw in my mother's eyes told me just how helpless she was feeling. I wanted to get better but I was sinking deeper into depression. If you have never been close to losing your mind, this may sound a little strange but I found solace in feeling numb and I slowly felt myself slipping away. It was only by the grace of God that I did not completely lose my mind. No matter how many people told me that I should be glad I had other children, it could not take away the emptiness left by the loss of my baby. It was the pained expressions that I constantly saw on the faces of my husband and children that made me realize just how close I was to having a nervous breakdown—I had far too much to lose.

Over time, I learned in the process of death, there is life. On my road to recovery, I would learn that though I had suffered loss, I was not a loser. I was battered, cracked and almost broken, yet none of this could hold me down. God assured me that I would never again suffer a stillbirth. My womb made me a breeding ground for dreams and miracles. Remember, life is never meant to stay the same. You may be in a winter season now but after you go through this bitter cold a season of spring will come and the sun will begin to shine in your life. You can make it to the next season, if you just hang in there.

Devastation

I so looked forward to celebrating my 40th birthday, a tremendous milestone in my life. I did not know that my mother's special tribute to me during my birthday service would be her last. Turning forty was going to be something different, I just did not know how different. The Wednesday following my birthday my daughters were taking me out for breakfast but all that morning I had this unexplainable longing to see my mother. I called and asked her to go out to eat with us and she did. That would be the last time I would see my mother alive. The telephone call I received from my aunt on that Saturday night was to let me know that my mother was having trouble breathing and had to be rushed by ambulance to the hospital.

After what seemed like forever, the doctor finally came out and told us that my mama had suffered a massive heart attack and had gone into cardiac arrest three times. He said the words that changed my life forever; the last time they brought her back she had been without oxygen to her brain for too long and was now in a coma. Nearly passing out, I felt like the wind had been knocked out of me. I was told she was going to need emergency surgery, but it was later determined that she did not have any brain activity and life support was the only thing keeping her alive. I was going to have to let her go...I would have to make the decision to pull the plug.

Who's That Woman in the Mirror?

She never even woke up from the coma, I never even got to say goodbye.

I thought losing my son was the hardest thing I ever had to go through, but the loss of my mama left me in total devastation. My grief was beyond me for my mother was the only consistent person I could remember my whole life and now she was gone. How could I live without my mama? This was an unfamiliar place but one I would get to know well. After losing my mother so unexpectedly, I suddenly began to fear that what happened to her would happen to me. I first went into denial that she had really died and then I cried for what seemed like forever. I guess it was during one of my crying spells that I realized I was angry with God for allowing this to happen to me. I had to be honest because He knew my heart anyway. I felt such a hole inside of me and I did not ever think I would heal.

I thought about death so much that I had forgotten how to live. You must allow yourself the time you need to grieve because everyone grieves in his or her own way and the process differs for each individual. With my son, I felt I needed to heal right away for everybody else, but this time I did not care because I was hurting and this pain was too much for me to bear. How could I make a comeback after this? It was only when I began to live off the good memories, that I was able to heal and live again.

I had been hit with some powerful knockdown punches and they nearly resulted in a "TKO". Each time I was knocked down, it took me deeper into the pit and almost swallowed me up. I refused to be defeated so I took a chance on a much happier ending to a story that had not been fully told. People will often count you out before they see how your story really ends. You too may have been knocked down, but you can get back up again. I have found comfort in Galatians 6:9 (KJV), "And let us not be weary in well doing: for in due season we shall reap, if we faint not."

There are some women who tend to hide behind masks so that no one will ever know who they really are and they do not like who they have become. I will no longer live my life behind a mask because I do not fear being transparent anymore. We can be strong for everyone else but not for ourselves. When we are hurting, we must be careful not to hurt others. There is an old familiar proverb that says, "hurting people, hurt people". The pain should not be an excuse but it should keep us from putting unrealistic expectations on those we love.

What I endured was a blessing in disguise. Had I not gone through those rough times, I am not sure that I would be the confident woman I am today. Life is all about difficulties, joy and pain, sunshine and rain—but your attitude is what determines your altitude through it all. I not only found peace, but I enjoyed finding the real me in the process. I am a woman with a poise and faith in God and I am absolutely convinced that it will be worth it all in the end.

You may never fully comprehend how your setback can become a setup for your comeback. God will enable you to make the best out of the worst situations in life. I discovered that I am not a weak woman, but I am a woman who has weaknesses. I want every young girl, every teenager and every woman who has had their share of pain to know that the fact that you are still standing means that your life has a purpose. Live everyday like it is your last, love everyone as if it is the last time you will see them—spread joy to someone else and you will find inner peace.

Who am I today? I am a woman who knows her worth. If you dare ask me that question again, my answer is still the same. I am the Queen of Comeback…I offer no regrets and no excuses for who I am. I am Undoubtedly, Unequivocally, Unashamedly…Unapologetically Woman!

Reflections by Fertamia (Tammy) Smith

The Power to Forgive
Even for the most horrific abuse…

So many years I have walked around with shame, not knowing how to relieve the pain. No one could help me until I found God. He has helped me, healed me and now I am free.

So many women out there harbor a hidden secret that they do not want to talk about with anyone. Some women cannot even tell their husbands, and their husbands walk around not knowing why their women do not want to be touched, or bothered "in that way."

I will confess for all of them: I was 14Yrs old when I was raped. I was also a virgin, so I lost a part of me twice in that one painful night. For many years, I was the one to blame; in my mind it was all my fault.

Nevertheless, today—I am healed, I am a survivor! If I would have lost myself, that mean person that stole my precious jewel would have won. By staying true to the Word, going to church and trusting in God (not man), I am able to make it. I hold my head up high as I gather my stride and realize that healing is a day-by-day process.

I finally saw the man that took my virginity through rape the other day, and I walked up to him with a smile and I told him, "I FORGIVE YOU." Oh my God… what a weight lifted from me after all of these years! That man was a part of my life for so long and I did not even know it. I understand now the power to forgive… Thank you God for Deliverance.

Section Four
The Power of Life in Spite of My Right Now!

Foreword for Christina Chlopecki

As the Pastor of Potter's House Christian Fellowship Church in Chicago, IL., I am honored to write a foreword for Christina's chapter. When I came to the Potter's House eighteen months ago after a year of missionary work in Malaysia, Christina was an active member who was already enriching our congregation with her many talents. She has not only designed our evangelism literature and bulletin boards, but she also plays the flute and sings in the service. Christina's generous spirit is always on display as she gives several church members rides to and from church services.

Over the past year, I have witnessed Christina's enduring faith in her struggle with all the adjustments that come with a heart transplant. Even though she has had to spend much time in the hospital, Christina's joy and tremendous faith has carried her victoriously through it all. You will be amazed by Christina's story of her health challenges, but I am sure you will be more inspired by her spirit.

Pastor Charles Baker
Potter's House Christian Fellowship Church

Christina Chlopecki

Christina is a 25-year-old freelance graphic designer who resides in Chicago, IL. On March 16th, 2008, after four months of waiting, Christina was blessed with the marvelous gift of a heart transplant and a second chance at life.
Christina is a devoted Christian who enjoys being involved in music, drama and other arts ministries at her church in Chicago, IL. Her passion is sharing her testimony on the streets and evangelizing at various churches and events. She is also passionate about helping others to obtain salvation by spreading the Gospel of Jesus Christ.

I Can Breathe Again
By Christina Chlopecki

I have very few memories of my father, for I was only three years old when he suffered a stroke and died. At only twenty-five years old at the time, my poor father was very ill. He had been suffering from a very rare heart disease and he needed lungs and a new heart. One memory I do have is from the funeral wake, when I asked my father for a piece of gum while looking down at him in his casket.

After my father passed away, my mother had three other children, one girl and two boys. Although my siblings were all very healthy, my mother always had a strange fear and suspicion that I might have possibly inherited the rare heart condition from my father. Throughout grade school, I was fairly healthy and was active academically and physically. I participated in numerous after school programs like dance, band, and Girl Scouts. During those years, I remember my mother taking me on special train rides to Cook County Hospital where I would "just get checked out." Other than an irregular heartbeat, there were no abnormal or concerning results; the doctors always concluded that I was a "very healthy girl."

The Power of Life in Spite of My Right Now!

It was not until high school that my own heart problems began. During my freshman year, I collapsed in gym class after my teacher ignored my doctor's note and insisted I run ten laps around the football field in 90-degree weather. Later that day, my mother took me to Loyola Hospital in Maywood to see a cardiologist. He examined me and did an echocardiogram—an ultra sound test to gather specific information about the size of the chambers and the heart's pumping function. The doctor soon discovered that I had an enlarged heart and after reviewing my father's medical history and health records, my doctor observed that my EKG was remarkably similar to my father's records. Because of the strong similarities, the doctor explained that I too might eventually need a heart transplant but for the time being, I could resume regular daily activities.

A few years later, when I was twenty-one I passed out again and this time, I woke up in the hospital. The doctors said my heart was racing uncontrollably and I would have to be monitored daily. Eventually, they inserted a pacemaker/defibrillator, under my left shoulder to shock me whenever my heart rate went past 180. The first time it worked, I was on a treadmill at the gym. A woman on the treadmill next to me had begun running at a fast pace embarrassed by how slowly I was walking in comparison, I tried to speed up just a little bit. All of a sudden, the treadmill shut down as a shock went through my entire body from head to toe! My heart rate had gone up triggering the pacemaker to jolt me! Thinking I was having a heart attack, I screamed out but fortunately, everyone in the gym had on earphones and they did not hear me. Suddenly, I felt weak and nauseous my hands were shaking badly. I was so embarrassed and distraught by the incident that I just picked up my things and went home.

Over time, my physical conditioned worsened and so did my emotional state; every day it was getting harder to breathe and harder to function in life. I started to get depressed because I did not have the energy I had before even though I was a very young women. I was unable to enjoy the simple pleasures of life that I once knew and loved so well and my entire life as I knew it was crashing down on me. I dreaded any type of physical activities with my friends. Although I used to enjoy dancing, it became too much for me to handle. If we took the train downtown, I could not even the climb stairs or keep up with my friends; I was always lingering in the back just trying to keep up.

During my sickness, I was also in an unhealthy relationship that took a huge toll on my health as well. My depression got so bad that I started to lose my memory. The lack of concentration made daily tasks at work harder to do, and I would even get lost driving. My bills were piling up too, but the thought of running back home to my family was out of the question. As each day went by, I grew more miserable and life

The Power of Life in Spite of My Right Now!

became unbearable, as I was not happy. Searching for a way out, I even contemplated suicide. I held off on calling my doctors, not knowing that I was actually dying.

Later, I did start seeing a psychiatrist for stress. One particular night I was drained after three days of not sleeping, I cried out to the Lord for the first time in my life. On my knees, I sobbed and felt embarrassed to even call out to Him under the circumstances, yet I knew I needed help. I had no other options, so I cried out, "Lord, if you really are real, please show me. Help me believe in you because I don't know what else to do." I continued to sob for about five minutes on my living room floor all of a sudden; I felt a wave of peace sweep over me. In my heart, I felt like everything was going to be all right. I did not understand the whole concept of how God answers prayers, but I was overjoyed to get some peaceful sleep that night finally.

The next day, I was out with my girlfriend at the Puerto Rican Festival in Chicago and I will never forget the phone call that stopped me dead in my tracks. "How did you get this number?" I asked the caller on the other end of the line. "I found your resume on your College website. I called your old residence and your uncle gave me this number. Can you come in for an interview tomorrow morning?" the man asked. "Of course I can, see you tomorrow at nine!" I replied. I was too embarrassed to tell my friend about my prayer the very night before the call. To some, it would seem that the telephone call came out of nowhere but I knew it was God's doing, his way of showing me that he was indeed real. Chills ran up my spine the more I thought about all of this. The following day, I got ready for my interview; confident that this was God's plan; I drove to the address that I knew would soon be my new place of employment. During the interview I told the man behind the desk, "I don't know if you believe in God or not, but I know this is where He wants me planted. I prayed for this to happen and God answered my prayers. I want to be honest with you, I am sick and I do have many doctors' appointments coming up… but I promise you I will never lie to you and I'm a hard worker."

I was not surprised when I was offered the job and it was absolutely perfect! I could not believe I had landed my dream job; just a few weeks before, I had been daydreaming about working for a huge advertising company downtown. Now there was no need to dream anymore, there I was working on creating advertisements for successful magazine companies like *Seventeen* and *Pageantry*. A few days after getting my new job, I received an email from an old friend inviting me to his church but I laughed and paid it no mind because I remember how this guy used to mock me whenever I mentioned God to him. Then he called me one night and I heard his sincerity on the phone, "you HAVE to come to this church,

The Power of Life in Spite of My Right Now!

Christina! I can really feel God in this place!" He sounded very convincing.

"What's the name of this place anyway?" I asked.

"The Potter's House," he replied.

A few days passed and I really had not put much thought into going to church. I figured I did not really need church because I could pray at home and God could answer my prayers. One day I got lost driving again. I can remember a certain sign that struck me because it read "POTTER." I ended up passing by that sign three times that day so I called my friend to ask for the church address to.

When I walked in, it sure did not feel like any church I had ever been to; it was very small and I didn't see a big cross on the wall, but I felt the presence of God immediately. It was a weird feeling to me and I really did not pay any attention to anyone else in the church. I was just listening to the words of the Pastor, it sounded like he was talking about me and I almost got mad at my friend. "Had my friend said something to Pastor about me?" I wondered. That was when I first learned what it means to feel conviction. At the end of the service, the Pastor prayed and with our heads bowed, he asked if there was anyone who wanted to give their life to Christ and be forgiven of their sins. Unashamed, I raised my hand, walked up to the altar, and prayed with one of the sisters in the church. I immediately felt like a brand new person upon accepting Christ.

Things started to get much better for me as I began going to church regularly. I even returned to college full-time to complete my Bachelor's Degree. My new job was working out well and I had more than enough money to live on my own. I was a bit stressed from all of my new responsibilities, but my prayers were being answered one by one. Still, I never took the time to truly seek God's word or what He commanded of me. I hardly ever prayed, I only prayed when I needed something from God.

During that time, I noticed that my friends were hanging around me more often. I had the extra money to spend and I did not mind blowing it off on foolish thinks like clubs, drinking and clothes. Soon, I pretty much wore myself down; my daily activities were occupied by work and school. Work stretched into twelve-hour days, and then I would go home to spend hours on homework. I would fall into bed at four a.m. to be back up at seven. On weekends, I would still try to hang out with my friends, "being the loyal friend that I was." Then off to church I went on Sundays, which was ridiculously hard to sit through because I was hung over from the previous night partying.

The day came when my health got so bad that I could not even climb a flight of stairs or walk through the grocery store.

The Power of Life in Spite of My Right Now!

I was constantly holding my stomach from the pain and I thought I was just retaining water so I still did not call my doctor. One day I finally picked up the phone and called my cardiologist. "Something is wrong and I can't breathe or walk," I said to her on the phone. That same night, I was admitted into the hospital; a little scared and nervous, I had no idea what was ahead of me. I was in denial and made up excuses for why I was feeling so tired and worn out. I refused to think I was as sick as I was. As far as I knew, I thought the doctors just wanted my money and I got tired of paying medical bills. It seems I heard a million voices in my head but none of them could answer why I was going through all of sickness.

The following day, the doctor did a biopsy of my heart to see how it was functioning; the surgery was painful and scary. I held my breath throughout the entire test afraid that if I breathed too hard it would be even more painful. At the end of the test, my hands were shaking and I could not believe they kept me awake throughout the entire procedure. When they rolled me out of surgery, my mom was waiting for me. Tears flowed from my eyes but I still could not let out a real cry from being so traumatized.

Doctors and nurses surrounded my bedside as they gave me the terrible news. "Christina, your heart is failing. The blood is not flowing to your brain properly and if you do not get a heart transplant soon, you will die. You will not be going home until you receive a transplant. You will be in the heart transplant unit, isolated from the rest of the hospital. We had no idea how serious your heart condition was… I know this is a lot to take in right now, I'm really sorry." All the doctors trailed off whispering to one another. My tears were flowing freely now and the room was spinning—what about my new apartment? What about my new career? What about my LIFE…this wasn't happening to me! Here I was going through the same thing my father went through at the same age of twenty-five.

My mom held my hand and kissed me for comfort. She left to grab a bite to eat as I lay awake staring at the ceiling for hours. This had to be a nightmare, I'll wake up from it soon, I was sure of it. However, I never awoke from the nightmare because it was real and happening.

Night after night, I woke up in the same room for months. Hearing machines beeping throughout the night drove me insane. The four a.m. blood draws were really fun; wires and machines attached to me pumping medicines into my body to keep me alive. I got sponge baths because I was too weak to stand for long periods of time, it just wasn't fair. "Lord, what did I do to deserve this?" I thought for sure the Lord was punishing me and I was feeling very low those first few weeks. To make matters worse, my Uncle Jimmy, who spent his life devoted to the Lord, passed away as soon as I got saved. I believe that I was the last person he spoke to before he died. He had called me to say, "Teena, I'm so glad you gave your heart to the Lord, I love you so much."

The next day, his brother, my Uncle Mike, came to the hospital to tell me that Uncle Jimmy had passed away. My heart was broken as I sobbed in my uncle's arms. Uncle Mike looked pale and sick himself because both of his brothers were now gone, along with his parents (my grandparents) and his first-born son. I was the last one he had left on our side of the family and things were not looking too good for me at that point. Pastor called me one night and said, "Christina I don't want you to think you did anything to deserve this. One day you'll have all the answers to why this happened." He prayed with me and kept me encouraged. Family members, friends and people from my church filled my room with flowers and gifts, some people who hardly knew me showed me such love and compassion. I also notice that those the friends with whom I had spent so much of my time and money with hardly ever called; they just continued to live their lives without me. By then, I was not angry with them, I was angry with myself for giving so much my time and energy to such foolish things. I almost drove myself crazy wondering what I could have done differently.

I turned to reading the Bible for encouragement and God really began to speak to me. I discovered how forgiving our Father really is and what I could do to really start serving him. Night after night, I prayed and read His word as I drew very close to the Lord. I promised Him that if He gave me a second chance I would devote the rest of my life to Him. God really delivered me there in that hospital and really changed my heart. I turned from being angry and feeling sorry for myself to being grateful that God provided a place I could be cared for. God showed me miracle after miracle in that hospital. For example, there was a period where I was unable to eat for two weeks; I just could not keep down any food. I was so sick that I did not even want to stay awake. People stopped visiting as much because it was so hard to watch me get sicker. I lost so much weight and there was no color in my face as I grew weaker and weaker. Pastor came to the hospital with an evangelist one day, both of them laid hands on me and prayed for me to be able to eat again. By the end of the night, I was eating again; the nurses discovered that my problem had stemmed from retaining water in my stomach. I was in tears as I called my Pastor excitedly to tell him his prayers had been answered.

Waiting for a heart can take a long time; I can even remember one call was a false alarm, when I thought they had found a potential donor heart. Later, I was told that the heart was not the right size; it was heartbreaking, no pun intended! The doctors then explained that I really needed a child's heart because I was so petite. Although my blood type B negative, was not considered rare, it was very difficult to get a small heart donor. The heart had to be the perfect size for me and in perfect condition because my doctor was not going to settle for anything that was less than perfect.

The miracle call finally came on March 16, 2008 when my mom, sister and brother were visiting me at the hospital. It was Palm Sunday to be exact and we were all so excited; but I could tell my family was also very scared. The closer it got to my surgery, the more family members filled my room making it hard for me to continue to smile and say, I will be okay; but what else could I do? Most of the girl relatives were screaming and crying, I was trying to listen to the doctors as they described the transplant procedure they had been preparing for the last four months. My Aunt Rose, the strongest woman that I know, was crying so hard; I had seen this woman fight with men and girls, but I had never seen her cry. She was so strong, she never cried in front of anyone until that day. I held back tears as I reassured my family that I was in God's hands—I was ready to get this over with, I was ready to get on with my life and ready to get out of the hospital. If anything were to go wrong, I was already prepared for the worst, I was ready to stand before God.

As they rolled me into the operating room, I heard the cries get louder. They turned on some music for me and I begged them to make sure I was asleep—my eyes closed and the surgery began. Twelve hours later, I awoke from the surgery strapped down to the recovery bed. I could not move my hands or even talk because there were tubes in my mouth. The doctors had gone over what I could expect before my surgery so I did not panic. I looked around and the first thing I noticed was the clock on the wall but I had no idea what day it was. The nurse came and pulled the tubes out of my mouth. My first statement was, "Praise God!" the nurse said, "What honey?" I said, "Praise God, now please get my mother!" She ran off and I saw my mom walk into the room.

God had truly performed a miracle in my life! Not only was I blessed with a new heart physically, I was also blessed within my spirit. Since my illness, I now know my purpose for living is to reach out to as many lost souls as I can with God's Word and His guidance so they may live life according to His standards and walk in His love. During my illness, God taught me so much about faith and forgiveness. He humbled my heart by breaking me down and then "He placed my feet on solid ground" once again.

Within the last year, my new heart has grown stronger and I can now live life in fullness and peace. It feels like the blinders have been taken off me and now I can live in this world with confidence and faith that God is with me no matter what. I do not care about what the doctors proclaim my future to be, right now I am living a healthy clean life, and walking with God. I have never felt so peaceful! Whenever the devil tries to discourage me or knock me down, I stand on the promise in Matthew 19:26 (NIV) that, "with man this is impossible, but with God all things are possible." I will always remember that when I had no power of my own, God made a way for me to get a new heart and now, I am finally able breathe again!

Foreword for Marilynnette Barney

I will never forget walking down that long, cold corridor; all I could hear was the sound of my very own footsteps as my shoes clicked against the white tiled floors. The noise of the steel doors shutting behind me made me realize it was all real and not a dream. I left my friend, my sister, my spiritual daughter locked behind bars; bars from which only God Almighty could release her. Leaving her there was more than I could bear...I felt so helpless. No matter how hard I prayed, she would become part of a world and a system that would change the dynamics of her life forever. What I knew for sure was that my friend, my sister, my daughter would emerge victorious because of her undying faith and trust in God.

Pastor Joyce Dennis,
Rhema Family Worship Center

Marilynnette Barney

Marilynnette is a community activist and has served as a mentor for the Cook County Juvenile Court system of Chicago, IL. She holds as B.A. in Urban Ministry and has committed her life to helping pastors move their ministries to the next-level.

Marilynnette currently teaches a bi-weekly empowerment class at New Life for Girls, helping women to move beyond their painful past(s) to realize their full potential in Christ. Passionate about God's daughters, Marilynnette ministers to women from all walks of life.

Anointed for this day and time to fulfill the call that has been placed upon her life, Marilynnette answered this call long before becoming a Minister. Marilynnette is a Chicago, IL., resident. She accepted Jesus Christ in 1981 and is an Elder at Rhema Family Worship Center.

Trial by Fire
By Marilynnette Barney

Have you ever gone through an ordeal so traumatizing that you found yourself wondering, "Where are you, God? Why am I a Christian? Did I miss it? God, are you punishing me?" You are not alone. I am convinced that during our Christian journey we all have experiences that shake us to the core and make us evaluate our lives. My traumatic experience came after I had been saved for twenty-one years; I became convinced then that being a Christian never exempts you from bad experiences. Bad things do happen to good people; the judge used those very words at our sentencing.

During this traumatic ordeal, I came across a portion of scripture that became the theme of my life story found in (1 Peter 4:12-19 KJV). It amazed me that God had already given us a heads up in His word—believers would experience trials and tribulations. The very first verse I Peter 4 says, "Forasmuch then as Christ hath suffered for us in the flesh, arm yourselves likewise with the same mind..." (KJV). Yes, I know what you are thinking, twenty-one years of being a Christian and you never read this scripture? I want to say, "No never," but the reality is that I had never had an occasion to really connect this truth to my life. Of course, I had heard down through the years the old saying; "Must Jesus bear the cross alone and all the world go free? No, there's a cross for you and for me." However, I was so naïve, I used to think that the "bearing the cross" had to do with not being able to pay your light bill or being sick. I never imagined that my cross could mean serving a prison sentence; for me, that just seemed a little farfetched.

It was 2002 when I faced the trial that would turn my world upside down; a journey that forever changed my life. I had not expected it but I knew that I had to go through it if God was going to use me as He planned before the foundation of the world. I even remember my young adult daughter poking fun at me back in those days before my ordeal, she used to say, "Aw mom, you don't understand, you never been through anything. You've been saved all your life." She felt I did not relate to what she was experiencing in life because I had never had a theodicy in my life to challenge my faith. Little did she know at the time that I was about to experience my own "trial by fire."

To be sure, the seeds of this trial were sown years earlier. Four years into my marriage my husband and I we were raising my daughter, my younger sister, as well as my husband's Godson. Although we did not have any children together at this point, I enjoyed being able to share our home with children. One day, I had the chance to talk at length with a friend who was a foster parent. After hearing about foster care, I realized that this was something my husband and I definitely wanted to do. We did the research, were screened, and received training to become foster parents. Then my husband and I were entrusted with the care of an eleven-year-old boy. This was not our ideal preference since we were hoping for a young child of two to three years old we could eventually adopt as our own, but we welcomed this older child into our lives. We were led to believe that we would soon receive a child in the age bracket we desired.

I really enjoyed being a mother and when God created this world, He gave five Kingdom principles for us to live by—to be fruitful, to multiply, to replenish, to subdue, and to have dominion. It is also my belief that when He created woman He put in her an innate desire to love, protect, and nurture children. A mother's love is really very special and something to contend with, because of this I knew I was blessed to be a mother to my 11-year-old foster son and to my great niece, my nephew's daughter. Since her birth, I had kept her on the weekends. Her mother was incarcerated when she was six years old so I became her full-time guardian. Truly, caring for these my children brought me great happiness.

Months and then years went by with no mention from the agency or any news of the little boy or girl we desired, a spirit of discouragement began to set in. Still, it did not hinder our love for the foster child we cared for even though he had many emotional needs. We spent countless hours with teachers, psychiatrists, and therapists to ensure his healthy development. We visited with his biological family and scheduled multiple visits to the agency trying to learn the best way to share love with our foster son who had been let down so many times before. In spite of all our efforts, it seemed as if all our foster son really wanted was the unconditional love of his biological mother.

Looking back now, I see how in all this a trap was being set. The devil had a demonic plan and he was forming a weapon to use against us. After trying time and again to address all our son's issues, I became worn and tired of the process. On the one hand, I wanted to return the child to the agency but I knew that was not a viable option. Who would return a child as if you would return a pair of shoes? I sincerely believed that there was healing for the emotional hurts that our son was facing so I held on to hope. I knew that just as Jesus had healed the man running naked through the graveyard that same healing was available to our son. We had put in many hours and a whole lot of love into this child, NO RETURNS! I even convinced my husband that we should care for him until he graduated from the eighth grade.

When his eighth grade graduation came, it was a joyous occasion. It was heartwarming to see how our son had excelled in areas that others said he would not. That got me thinking that maybe we should care for him until he graduated from high school. Then at least he would be able to live independently instead of being shipped to another foster home; reluctantly, my husband agreed. Early in his first year of high school, we noticed that our son was becoming more and more aggressive. At fifteen years old, he was experiencing a myriad of stresses—hormonal changes, adjusting to a new school, the bullying of other students, and dashed hopes that he would ever reunite with his biological family It was as if he was a time bomb waiting to explode. We were struggling to deal with his issues and we had very little help; even the agency seemed to have given up on him and had left us holding the bag.

Many times, we fail to realize that the enemy studies us from the day we are born and he learns our weak and strong areas. The devil had studied me and he knew that one of my weaknesses was letting go. I believe that the devil knew that if he was ever going to stop me from fully engaging in Kingdom work his time to act was now so he began to activate his plan to destroy me! I remember September 29, 2002 as if it were yesterday. That was the day the enemy had chosen to make his move! Within minutes, my once happy life was shattered. Our son had enjoyed a fun-filled day attending a birthday party at a local indoor amusement park. He was still excited when he came home so I was surprised when less than thirty minutes later he began acting out. When I confronted him, he became angry and aggressive. I sent him to his room to think about what he had done and he proceeded to follow me around with a balled up fist. I knew a fifteen-year-old male following me with his fist balled up meant trouble.

I turned around and told him, "Don't walk behind me like that. Go to your room!" I headed for my bedroom only to discover he was still behind me; this is not good, I thought. I rushed into my bedroom to wake my husband who was asleep in his recliner. I explained to him what was happening.
From that moment on, our lives turned upside down. All of a sudden, life truly became a nightmare as my husband and I experienced the criminal justice system firsthand. I had never ever imagined landing in County Jail, but I ended up somehow with an inmate number and a $50,000.00 bond. What had happened? God forbid my husband had broken the boy's bones or killed him… of course he had not. So why was I incarcerated?

I kept thinking this could not be happening; we were locked up for twenty-six days. During that time, the bond was reduced to $10,000.00 for each of us. With money collected from family, friends and employers, our bond was paid and we were released. Returning home, from jail I was emotionally devastated, I curled up in a fetal position underneath the covers and just rocked and rocked. I could not even get up out of bed, heart palpitating, blood pressure skyrocketing, my doctors were concerned. They said that I would surely die if I did not get control of whatever was going on in my head.

The weapon had been formed and the devil plans seemed to be working, but just then, God stepped in to the situation. I got a phone call from my mother, she had been watching Dr. Fred Price on Christian TV and he was instructing people to write all their issues and concerns on a sheet of paper, pray over them, tear them up, and throw them into the garbage. I figured that I had nothing to lose since doctors were saying I was going to die anyhow. Therefore, I did as I was instructed, I wrote everything down. My husband and I joined hands across the bed and we prayed. Several minutes later, I opened my eyes to find the paper gone. Oh, my God, what happened to it, I wondered. Little did I know that my husband had picked the paper up and threw it in the trash basket in our room. From that day on, I was never bothered with palpitations again and I began to get stronger physically and spiritually. I was in for a battle and I was ready to fight.

Women of God, we must always remember that the devil hates our seed and us; his job is to steal our plans and dreams, kill our purpose, and destroy us before we realize our potential and true worth on the earth. If we are ever get a hold to

The Power of Life in Spite of My Right Now!

who we really are, we would know that devil is intimidated by us and the authority we posses in God. We are capable of wreaking havoc in his kingdom of darkness. When I began to really understand my power, I began to discover who I really was in CHRIST!

My official court trial did not begin for three years and in that time, I had thirty-five court appearances. Surely, my faith was sorely tested as I was being re-built from the inside out. I had to learn to deal with prejudice, lies, and shame. It was as if a knife had been inserted in my back.

I had thought it was against the law to eavesdrop on someone in his or her home without permission. Therefore, I do not understand how a neighbor could have inadvertently recorded 300-400 hours of video activity in our home without being charged. It was as if the county did not care about our rights. In addition, unfortunately it was the word of a Caucasian woman versus the word of an African American husband and wife. Mind you, we lived in a nice home and had never had so much as traffic ticket, therefore you would think that our reputation as law-abiding citizens would count for something—but it did not!

At the end of our trial, we were found guilty and sentenced to serve time in the State of Illinois penal system, my husband received four years and I was sentenced to three and a half. I felt we had been unjustly accused and sentenced. How do you deal with injustice and still trust God? My real test of faith had only just begun. I found encouragement in the Word of God, Proverbs 24:10 says, "If thou faint in the day of adversity, thy strength is small" (KJV). I determined not to faint because I knew God would not abandon us while we were in prison. Looking back, I am so glad that the God we serve is able: I ended up serving only 10 months and my husband served just 14 months. Even if God had not delivered us, I never doubted that He was able. When He brought me out of that fiery furnace, I did not even smell of smoke and I was freed of the residue from the past.

Today I am stronger, wiser and better because of what I went through because I know that it all was for the glory of God. Through all my adversity, God was refining my character—I was tried in the refiner's fire and I came out better once the impurities and flaws of my character were burned away. My gifts, talents, and character were developed. I came through the fire and emerged like pure gold.

Now God is honored as I touch the lives of other women with His anointing that flows through me. Truly, I have discovered the courage to be a woman unapologetically and I refuse to live with guilt or regrets. I hope that as you read this book you discover that there is hope and strength in Christ to face all of life's battles.

The Power of Life in Spite of My Right Now!

My prayer is that you will always take a stand against the kingdom of darkness. When you wake up in the morning and before your feet hit the floor may the devil say, "Aww heck, she's up again?"

Foreword for Paulita Eskridge

Maya Angelou told us that a phenomenal woman has a stride in her step, an arch in her back, a grace in her style, and an unbowed head. The book of Proverbs teaches us that a virtuous woman's price is far above rubies. Her loins and arms are strong. Her mouth holds wisdom, her tongue the law of kindness, and her children call her blessed.

It is obvious that God has a love of poetry and personified these verses when He created Paulita. Through many situations which would have tested the mental strength of Einstein and the brawn of Samson, Paulita pulled through. She maintained dignity and walked upright. If she bowed her head, it was to pray for sustenance and give thanks to the Almighty. Even in the storms of life, Paulita has learned to waltz so gracefully through the rains, which are sometimes tears, until she reaches the sunlight, a rainbow, and the pot of gold. I feel honored to have been asked to write this foreword for Paulita as I have witnessed her faith, strength, endurance, and determination. She has been an inspiration and testimony to me during my own struggles.

Paulita...a phenomenal, virtuous, steel magnolia!

Tiffany Ford Townsend

Paulita Eskridge

Paulita graduated Summa Cum Laude with a Liberal Arts Degree from Concordia University in River Forest, Illinois. Paulita, a brilliant woman, is very down to earth. She has raised six beautiful children on her own. Paulita's life has been surrounded by shame, poverty, illness, and sorrow; but she never allowed any of these things to define the woman she has become. When you hear the words courageous and survivor, Paulita comes to mind. She inspires, motivates, and brings joy and empowerment to other women and everyone else she comes into contact with.

Paulita is a Christian, who has been a member of New Covenant Life Church under the leadership of Pastor John Hannah. Her faith in God and prayers are what sustain her.

Against All Odds
By Paulita Eskridge

To the triumphant anthem of Pomp and Circumstance, I walked down the aisle proudly for this was my special day! Finally, all my hard work had paid off and I was graduating Summa Cum Laude with my Bachelor's degree. Against all odds I had made it— running away from an abusive relationship, caring for six children as a single parent, and going to school while holding down a job. Against all odds, I had trusted God for His protection and healing. The joy I was experiencing that day was far removed from the fear and abuse I had endured for years at the hands of my boyfriend in order to get there.

I still remember the day I woke up in the hospital paralyzed from the waist down, my face was swollen, my eyes black and blue. The doctor had asked, "How did you get injured?" Fearing for my life, I claimed… "I fell down the stairs," it was a lie. Unfortunately, the doctor was too busy to read the terror in my eyes.

In the eyes of the world, I was a vibrant super mom. I was active in the community and in my children's lives. I worked part time as a dental assistant and a licensed hairdresser. Every week at church, I volunteered to help distribute food to the community while being a Girl Scout Leader and PTA mom. I took my children to choir rehearsal, drill team practice, and to their music, dance and tumbling lessons. On the face of things, we really appeared to be the ideal family. Yet, behind closed doors, I was suffering in an abusive relationship. The smallest thing would trigger my boyfriend's temper, sending him into violent rages. He was very possessive and volatile and I am still not exactly sure what caused him to pick me up and throw me across the room that fateful day. When I landed on top of the 25-inch color television, the room turned black. I woke later paralyzed for several weeks.

My boyfriend's aggressive behavior usually followed a predictable pattern. After several hours of drinking and doing drugs, he would become verbally, physically, and sexually violent towards me. To keep me quiet, he often threatened my life by convincing me that if I ever told anyone what was going on, he would kill me as well as my loved ones. I was so afraid of him, and I believed his threats to be true. Every day I woke up, I feared it would be my last, for I was sure that it was just a matter of time before he killed me.

One day, I felt God speaking to me, telling me to prepare to leave this abusive situation. Although I was apprehensive, I believed that God surely would protect me and provide for all my needs when I left. I began praying that He would keep me safe and I started putting together an escape plan from my fifteen-room home. The first thing I did was to secure a safety deposit box at a nearby bank. Since my boyfriend had a habit of hiding my purse from me, I hid one safety deposit box key at work and the other key I gave to a friend. Then I started storing important documents such as birth certificates, medical records, cash, copies of the keys for the house and car. I gathered information on storage fees, truck rentals, and the cost of an apartment. I knew I had to save as much money as I could to activate my plan.

Next, I gave all my children passwords for that the day when we would have to leave home in case of an emergency. I told them, "If you receive my "password" message, do not go home. Meet me or the person I send (with the password) at a designated place." I ended up activating my escape plan just a few weeks later. My boyfriend was about to leave for work and he was clearly upset about something. He had hidden my purse and car keys and then warned me to prepare for a beating when he got home. I felt an overwhelming sense of dread, I knew that if I did not leave the house that day, that I probably would die. So, in a moment of desperation, I decided to leave immediately!

For a brief moment, I prayed for God's protection as I hurriedly put my plan into action. I called the school and told

The Power of Life in Spite of My Right Now!

the secretary to give all my children an urgent message using the password. Then I called up a friend for a ride to meet my children at our designated meeting location. Since I barely had enough time to save enough money for an apartment, we had to go to a shelter. Unfortunately, there was no room for us at any of the shelters because of my family size. For several months, my children and I had to sleep at different places every night. Finally, by the grace of God, I was able to get us an apartment.

It was then that I decided to start all over again. Since I had quit my job of 14 years to insure our safety, I found a new part-time job and enrolled in five classes at a community college. Several months later, our family grew to include two more children. A friend of mine was unable to care for her children at the time and rather than have them go into foster care, I agreed to take in the two little girls, ages six weeks and three years old. I was already having a difficult time feeding my own four children, now I had six children to feed, clothe, and nurture. Not to mention, adding formula and diapers to a tight budget made having a newborn very expensive. To make matters worse, I could not get any assistance from welfare since I did not have legal custody of my friend's children. Besides, my income was just $7.00 over their financial limit so I did not qualify for any public aid benefits either way. I prayed to God many sleepless nights, pleading for food for my family and wisdom in those desperate days.

When I went to church, my eyes often filled with tears when people slipped me a $5 or $10 bill. I was always so thankful and appreciative for their gifts of love. Most felt their gifts were small but their donations really helped keep our family afloat. Usually, the money helped purchase a bag of diapers, a gallon of milk, a can of formula, lunchmeat and bread for the week. A few people even said, "The Lord told me that you needed this," and I realized my prayers were being answered, God was surely providing for us!

A year had passed by and just when we were all adjusting to our new lives, tragedy struck. One day while at work, I began to feel quite strange as if I was in a dreamy state of mind. I saw white flakes that no one else could see; I ignored the strange feelings because I was too busy. When I went into the bathroom to wash my flushed face, I could see the flakes coming back again. This time, the room seemed to be spinning and moving; and I was thinking why was everything turning cloudy and then black? Suddenly I could not see anything, but I could hear a lot of commotion around me. I heard sirens, then total darkness.

I awoke in the emergency room to doctors asking me questions and doing tests. When I was asked to walk across the room, I could not understand why my left leg was dragging. Although the most of the tests were simple, I failed every dexterity test. How could I fail such simple tasks?

The Power of Life in Spite of My Right Now!

The test results revealed that part of my brain was hemorrhaging and I needed immediate brain surgery. After the surgery, I had to relearn everything that most of us take for granted—how to walk, talk, and read. A physical therapist came to my home five days a week to help with my recuperation; there were good days and bad. One test revealed I was having seizures as I slept and I found it difficult to concentrate. My words did not come out as I desired and sometimes it was the complete opposite of what I was thinking. For example, if I were thinking, "turn left," the words would come out "turn right." To this day, I still find it difficult to pronounce certain words or use others in the proper context.

Looking back, I am so thankful for my family members who cared for me during my recovery of almost 2 years. Although I was still having difficulty with my concentration, I went back to work several months later. A year after returning to work, I re-enrolled in school. I was determined to complete my education because I knew I had to help my children. With all the negative influences out there, I definitely did not want them looking up to a drug dealer as a mentor. I knew that getting my education would be the open door to a better paying job. I wanted to be a positive influence and a mentor to my children! The verse that kept me going says- "And whatever you ask in prayer, you will receive, if you have faith" Matthew 21:22 (ESV).

Unapologetically Woman

I held on to God's word by faith and was inducted into the Phi Theta Kappa Honor Society graduating with my Associate Degree. Shortly afterwards, I enrolled into a private university but before the end of that first semester, I had to have another major surgery. During the surgery, the doctor accidentally ruptured my bladder. Within days of returning home, an infection developed and I had to be rushed back to the hospital--- within a week, I was diagnosed with breast cancer.

Once again, my family and friends extended their prayers and support. I looked to the scriptures for comfort: "They cried to the Lord in their trouble and He saved them out of their distresses. He sent His word, healed them, and delivered them from their destructions." (Psalm 107:19-20 NKJV) I knew my children needed me so I prayed for healing. Within two months, the cancerous cells were removed and I no longer had cancer. I did not need any necessary treatments afterwards… Amazingly, God healed me.

Upon my return to school, I was inducted into the Alpha Sigma Lambda National Honor Society for adult students. Within 18 months of my enrollment, I graduated with my Bachelors degree and was a Summa Cum Laude candidate.

I thought that the trials and tribulations of my life had subsided and I wanted to enjoy my life as a college educated young woman. Nothing could have prepared me for what was in store for me. One of a parent's worst nightmares is seeing their child seriously ill. Around Thanksgiving of 2007, it was determined that my daughter's heart was failing and that she needed a heart transplant. Too weak to go home, she had to stay in the hospital for an indefinite time until she received a donor heart from a baby or child. My daughter inherited the same disease that took the life of her late father. The flashbacks of his pain and suffering during the hospitalizations were unbearable. He was just 25 years old when I buried him; our daughter was three years old and our son just 15 months old.

During one of my visits, a nurse came into my daughter's hospital room and took away her food tray, which is a sign that they have a donor and they are going to prepare her for surgery. The next morning, on Psalm, Sunday March 16, 2008, she received her heart.

It was heartbreaking watching my child in so much pain after the surgery but within several weeks, the pain subsided. Praise God that my daughter was given another chance to live her life. However, we mourn for the family that lost their child. Although we do not know who the donor was, we knew that he/she had to be child or baby. We were told that my daughter's small body frame would only accept a small organ like from a child or baby. Much prayer and gratitude to the family for this wonderful gift during their time of loss. If you have not done so, please tell your relatives to become a donor. Give the gift of life.

Today I am a very grateful woman. Against all odds, I have survived. God has delivered me from domestic abuse, financial desperation, and powerful ailments that could have easily taken my life. Truly, I am a walking testimony of God's faithfulness and goodness!

No More Regrets

By Shameka Smith

Life is full of Regrets and Un-forgiveness!

Life is full of pain and heartaches!

Sometimes we must deal with ups and downs, trials and tribulations.

You have to get to the point when there will be no more procrastination.

I finally challenged myself to talk the talk and walk the walk.

What I mean is to stop talking about it, and just do it.

Looking into other peoples' lives did not change the person that I was.

I made the decision to make the necessary sacrifices to achieve my goals.

What are you going through?

In today's society people are going through a lot.

But, they have to choose not to let pride get in the way.

Dealing with today's situation, people are really going through a change.

It's either deal with it or not.

How do we deal with society?

How do we cope with what's surrounding us?

I found the answer!

Get Up! Help The World!

And help others change themselves, in doing so

We accomplish greatness and indeed, there are

No More Regrets!

Acknowledgements

Oh WOW! I can't believe that two years have already come and gone so quickly. I can remember working on another book and writing the words "Unapologetically Woman," in it and they just seemed to pop off the page at me. Now some two years later, eight women total have come together to share why they live life as women without regrets or excuses. I cannot take full credit for writing this body of work alone, I am especially grateful for all the readers, writers, and editors. This project has been a total act of faith; I have learned that a group of women can work together, without arguing or confusion.

To my co-authors, Juliet, Angela, Christina, Nicole, Marilynnette, Kim and Paulita, thank you so much for trusting me, with your investment, time, and writings. Many of you had never met me before this project. As a co-author with you, I am elated to share in such a Powerful and Empowering work, which I believe will literally help re-position women, as they align themselves with truth. I encourage you all to keep writing, and continue to be a "Light."

This body of work has been worked and re-worked overtime, to give our readers the essence of each woman's life. In my writings and dedication, I have mentioned my sister Fertamia "Tammy," who was scheduled to be one of our writers. Tammy is a woman who was scorned by lots of pain and sorrow, yet she was indeed a joy as a mother, sister, and friend.

I am so grateful that as a writer she documented her work and we have included some of her work in this project as "Reflections by Fertamia (Tammy) Smith," (Page 99).

Thank you honey and kids for being supportive of me during this time, as I have worked long hours planning and preparing for this wonderful project. I truly thank God for giving me such a wonderful vision and team to make the vision come alive.

I extend a special thanks to Shadrina Fleming of Fleming Admin Works for collaborating with EJF Publishing & Printing and making our books look fabulous! Thank you Shameka and Shadrina for your poems and to all those who have contributed Forewords and Reviews on behalf of all of the writers.

To my mom, Gloria, sweetheart I love you so much. You are such a sassy Queen and your sparkle makes me smile. Momma, you have really pushed me to finish this project, and I am so grateful you have, especially after losing Tammy. I am eternally grateful for you.

In closing, Ladies remember to live life as a woman of greatness, "Unapologetically Woman" always!

Collaboration Package

So, you would like to write?

EJF Publishing & Printing is always looking for aspiring authors. If you have the desire to get published but lack the funds or time to commit to a full book, we offer you the opportunity to participate in a book collaboration. Our collaboration process is exceptional.

As a collaborator, you are required to submit a chapter which supports the title of a book being published by **EJF Publishing & Printing.** Each writer then makes a small contribution financially and receives the reward of becoming a published author. We have recently completed our first collaboration and others are on the way.

Through our collaboration process:

- Writers connect and network with other writers
- Writers receive professional writing concepts and tips
- An excerpt of your writing is featured on our website
- Your chapter is professionally edited
- Graphic design services
- Chapter Formatting
- And more…

For more information on becoming one of our writers, please contact us via email at contact@ejfpublish.com or visit us on the web at www.ejfpublish.com.

EJF Publishing & Printing
Introduces
Papatha THE Adventurer
_{TM}

Papatha is a seven-year-old African American girl who is very adventurous and unique. Her nickname is affectionately "Pap." She has a puppy, his name is Leon and he is fluffy and brown with white and orange spots. Papatha is a very intellectual, fun, and adventurous child. She is always on a mission to try new things, and help someone all in the name of fun.

Papatha and her friends introduce learning skills in a unique way to assist with academic, social and cultural development.
Although, Papatha is not always right, she tends to think she is because she is very independent. Every child can identify with the early stages of gaining their independence and trying to learn new things. Papatha's character embraces all cultures and disabilities.

Books are sold in full color.

www.ingramcontent.com/pod-product-compliance
Lightning Source LLC
Chambersburg PA
CBHW031253290426
44109CB00012B/561